The Shakespeare Audition

THE APPLAUSE ACTING SERIES

The Shakespeare Audition

How to Get Over Your Fear, Find the Right Piece, and Have a Great Audition

Laura Wayth

Applause Theatre and Cinema Books
An Imprint of Hal Leonard Corporation

Published in 2015 by Applause Theatre & Cinema Books
An Imprint of Hal Leonard Corporation
7777 West Bluemound Road
Milwaukee, WI 53213

Trade Book Division Editorial Offices
33 Plymouth St., Montclair, NJ 07042

Printed in the United States of America

Book design by John J. Flannery

Library of Congress Cataloging-in-Publication Data
Wayth, Laura.
 The Shakespeare audition : how to get over your fear, find the right piece, and have a great audition / Laura Wayth.
     pages cm -- (The Applause acting series)
 Includes bibliographical references and index.
 ISBN 978-1-4950-1080-4
 1. Acting--Auditions. I. Title.
 PN2071.A92W39 2015
 792.02'8--dc23
                              2015028675

www.applausebooks.com

For my mom and dad

Contents

Acknowledgments

Special thanks to Stephanie Ann Foster, Shakespeare teacher extraordinaire and one of the best researchers I know, for contributing the chapter Finding Your Match.

Thanks also to my colleague David Meldman, for his contribution of research questions on Shakespeare's histories. Many thanks to Professor Bruce Avery, San Francisco State University, for his assistance.

Thank you to all of the wonderful teachers I have had in my career, and to my students, who teach me every day.

The
Shakespeare
Audition

Introduction

*A*uditions stink.

There. I said it. They really do.

And the only thing more daunting and nerve-racking than a regular old audition is an audition where it seems like you cannot connect with the material. Any audition that makes you feel like the text is somehow beyond your reach or foreign from your experience or understanding is a truly intimidating event.

We've all been there.

Classical auditions especially Shakespeare auditions are a fact of actor life. Theatre seasons often call for them. Graduate auditions require them. If you're a stage actor, you really need to do them. If they scare you, you're not alone.

My friend Jake, a professional actor in New Orleans, used to be terrified of Shakespeare.

"I was scared to death of anything even remotely Shakespearean," he confessed to me on the phone one day. "I didn't have the slightest idea how to begin to tackle it. It was hard to find meaning that I could relate to in the text. Every time I tried to give it life, it fell flat."

My friend Jenna, an actor in New York, had a similar experience. "I used to be terrified of Shakespeare for one reason: I felt stupid speaking his lines. When I was alone or messing around with friends I'd speak the lines with lots of energy and have fun and not care, but every time you put me in front of a class, a teacher, a director or an audition . . . it was a no-go."

My friend Paige, a Florida-based actor, had a similar response. "I always had respect for Shakespeare and appreciated the work from afar, but I never really understood it. I was just not comfortable speaking the language."

Each of these actors was scared of Shakespeare and of classical text. Each regarded Shakespeare's language as something foreign and strange. Each had difficulty finding meaning in the text and connecting to it personally.

Because of this discomfort, all three of these talented actors stayed home from very valuable auditions.

What if I told you that Shakespeare text really isn't all that scary or difficult? In fact, what if I told you that your classical-text audition could be every bit as fun, exciting, and vibrant—maybe even more so—than your contemporary-text audition? What if I gave you some guidance in selecting good classical material? What if I told you that I could help you find ways to understand and connect to this material personally and to make it your own?

What if I told you that you would never have to shy away from another classical-text audition again or go into one feeling less than confident?

Well, that's what I'm telling you. We can do this! And it will be easy and fun.

Let's get started.

1. Fear of the Bard
(and Why What Makes You Scared
Is What Should Make You Excited . . .)

I kind of hate calling him "The Bard," don't you? But that's what people often call Shakespeare. In medieval Gaelic and British culture, a bard was a professional poet employed by a patron (be it a monarch or nobleman) to write. Shakespeare is called *The* Bard because many people consider him the greatest poet that ever lived. And the idea that Shakespeare is first and foremost a *poet* is important for us to think about.

You see, the thing that probably makes you afraid of Shakespeare is the very thing that makes Shakespeare easy and fun. *Shakespeare is poetry.*

Although Shakespeare wrote prose, the majority of his work is in verse, aka poetry. Poetry has a specific shape and structure. Poetry has some rules governing the way it's created. Once you learn those rules and that structure, Shakespeare begins to make perfect, exquisite sense! The rules that shape the creation of poetry give the actor a kind of roadmap to follow. Learn how to read the map, and the road to Shakespeare-land rolls out before you and your performance springs to life. Once you understand the form, you unlock the key to actor fun and freedom. I'm going to give you an idea of how to do this in a little while.

But first, let's talk a little more about this dreaded P word—poetry. It sounds so formal, doesn't it? It seems like something reserved for Valentine's Day, or something archaic, ancient, and separate from our own experience. It seems fancy and formal and not how we express our truth. The biggest complaint I get from students who are new to Shakespeare when they speak his words goes something like this: "But I just don't feel like I'm being honest." This is the single biggest problem actors have in approaching Shakespeare—they just don't feel truthful speaking his words. And being truthful, after all, is the thing we actors value the most. To not feel truthful on stage is to feel fake, fraudulent, disconnected, self-conscious, and downright get-me-off-the-stage wrong.

But let's think of it another way. Poetry isn't our normal, everyday kind of truth. Poetry is greater than that. It offers an uplifted, larger-scale truth connected to all of humanity and to the divine. It isn't the way we speak—it's bigger and more powerful. So let's think of poetry like an even greater revelation of our thoughts and of ourselves. Let's think of it like music.

A song or a piece of instrumental music can take us to a place that is emotionally poignant and full of energy, encapsulating human experience even better than ordinary speech could. Music contains images. It is dense with a kind of information that we can understand not only on an intellectual level, but viscerally. Music can communicate what speech alone cannot. A violin can sing what someone's heart is feeling. A driving rhythm can capture all that is raw and primitive in our individual or collective experience. A soaring line can lift us up. A minor key can bring us to a down and dark place. Poetry does this. And poetry does this because poetry *is* a kind of music.

Poetry, like music, is heightened.

Let's look at the definitions for this great, beautiful, magic word, *heightened*:

transitive verb
1   a: to increase the amount or degree of : augment
    b: to make brighter or more intense : deepen
    c: to bring out more strongly : point up
    d: to make more acute : sharpen
2   a: to raise high or higher : elevate
    b: to raise above the ordinary or trite
3   *obsolete*: elate

intransitive verb
1   *archaic*: grow, rise
2   a: to become great or greater in amount, degree, or extent
    b: to become brighter or more intense (Merriam-Webster 2015)

I love all of these definitions, and they all apply to our friend Shakespeare. You see, Shakespeare's text is often called "heightened text." What is heightened text? Well, it's any text that contains and is driven by any or all of the wonderful definitions you see above. *Heightened text is a text that is elevated above daily, ordinary speaking. Heightened text has rhythmic structure and relies on imagery to deliver its meaning. It has a kind of density—a density not only of image, but of thought and emotion.*

When we start to see that Shakespeare shouldn't sound like we do in our everyday lives, but that Shakespeare should sound like we do when something in our lives is vitally, critically, amazingly important, we realize it's okay for us to be big on stage, and for us to be robust, dynamic, energetic, and ignited in our work. This heightened way of being and speaking Shakespeare's poetry is not at all untruthful, but a new, wonderful, refreshing, and vibrant "heightened" kind of truth.

The minute we can truly understand and accept this as actors is the minute when Shakespeare's truth and our truth align. Acting problem number one, solved!

The second reason actors fear Shakespeare, besides the fear that poetry somehow equates to a lack of honesty, is this: It's Shakespeare.

Oh, "Shakespeare" with a capital "S." Oh, my friends, the great onus of playing Shakespeare. You will do it "wrong," you think to yourself. "Everyone who has gone before me has done it better," you say. "I have no right to speak these words," you moan. "I can't possibly understand its greatness," you lament into your pint of ice cream. "And I'm already at a deficit because I don't have a British accent."

To all of this I say, "Nonsense!" (and I say it without a British accent). We have this strange idea that Shakespeare is supposed to sound or be a certain way, or else we're doing it wrong.

Not true. Shakespeare and his writing have endured for all of these years for one very big reason: his work, more than that of any other writer I can name, speaks to all of us. Shakespeare's characters and his writing are as true and as real to us today as they were in Elizabethan England. Some of the references may be unfamiliar, and some of the words may be archaic to the modern ear, but the characters, the issues they face, the questions they ask, and the feelings they experience strike a truthful chord across space and time with all of us. It is because Shakespeare wrote to and for all of us that we all—every last one of us—have a right to speak his words with our own experiences and our own understanding. Shakespeare is not some ancient thing behind glass in a museum. It is a living, breathing body of human truths. It is your job, right, and privilege to tell his stories from your own heart and mind.

Let's recap for a minute:

- Shakespeare is easy and fun because it has a poetic structure that, once you come to understand it, takes you, the actor, on a ride with it.
- Shakespeare is incredibly easy to relate to because he wrote with an understanding of the human condition that transcends time and culture.
- Shakespeare allows us—actually requires us—to be big and bold and to embrace language as a kind of music.

This is all the stuff that actors dream of, isn't it?

But there is even more great news for your Shakespeare audition, and it is this practical fact: it is really pretty darn easy to memorize the language quickly.

I have a callback tomorrow for a theatre in San Francisco. I have two pages of contemporary dialogue to memorize and my brain, preoccupied with teaching, grading, writing, and medicating my geriatric cat, is full. It can't quite hang on to the lines reliably on such short notice.

A few months ago, with even more going on in my life and with even less time to prepare, I had to get a chunk of Shakespeare's epic poem *Venus and Adonis* under my belt. I had it memorized in two days with very little effort.

This phenomenon, I believe, occurs for two reasons. The first: poetry is just easier to memorize. Your brain latches on to it with minimal effort. Why do you think television and radio commercials use musical jingles? They stick with you. You know how you can't get that annoying song out of your head? It's the same principle. All things musical—poetry being a musical thing—are easier to remember than nonmusical things. This is great news when it comes to auditions. How many times have you auditioned with flubbing your lines your chief worry and preoccupation? I go into half of my auditions more worried about line recall than my acting choices, which is really not the way it should be. Not so with Shakespeare. He made it easy!

The second reason: good writing makes sense. The play I have a callback for tomorrow (which shall remain nameless) has stinky writing, my friends. The thoughts don't track logically. The text repeats itself. It jumps around. One idea does not morph into the next. It slips out of my mental grip. Shakespeare is so beautifully written that every thought flows from the previous thought. Everything is connected. Connected writing moves along effortlessly. Connected writing makes your job a cinch.

Getting the text in your body with greater ease and connecting to that text easily means that with memorization squared away, you have more freedom to play.

What an idea—actually having the freedom to *play* in your audition! No racking your brain to think of the next line, no working overtime to try to weave together the thoughts and carve out a journey. The playwright has done the bulk of the work for you. It is simply your job to play. And isn't that what theatre is really all about and why we love to do it? We're *playing*!

And trust me—there's nobody more fun to play with than Shakespeare.

Hopefully you're getting a little excited about this now. I am.

2. Poetry, Prose, and All That Jazz

So, before we get into the really fun stuff—choosing your piece and learning how to play with it—let's look at a few things about the text that will help us to get a better sense of our framework before we dive in.

I've talked a lot so far about poetry. But I also mentioned that Shakespeare wrote prose, too.

How do you tell the difference between poetry and prose? And can it be poetry if it doesn't actually rhyme?

So to start with, let's define poetry. Poetry/verse, as we have said, is heightened language. We said that it is a kind of writing that is arranged to create a specific emotional response through meaning, sound, and rhythm and contains concentrated images. But what distinguishes poetry from prose is that it has meter—that is, a systematically arranged and organized rhythm.

Poetry does not necessarily rhyme. The bulk of Shakespeare's poetry is written in a form called *blank verse*. I remember my first Shakespeare audition, shortly after the earth cooled (no, it wasn't really that long ago . . . it just feels like it). I was told to prepare a speech in "blank verse" and *I* was a blank! What did it mean? What was blank verse and how could I recognize it?

Blank verse is a kind of poetry that is written in a regular metrical form, but where the lines are unrhymed.

Here is an example of blank verse from *A Midsummer Night's Dream*, a small portion of a long monologue. In this speech Titania, the Fairy Queen, scolds her vengeful and childish husband, Oberon:

> These are the forgeries of jealousy;
> And never, since the middle summer's spring,
> Met we on hill, in dale, forest, or mead,
> By paved fountain or by rushy brook,
> Or in the beached margent of the sea,
> To dance our ringlets to the whistling wind,
> But with thy brawls thou hast disturb'd our sport.
> Therefore the winds, piping to us in vain,
> As in revenge, have suck'd up from the sea
> Contagious fogs; which, falling in the land,

> Hath every pelting river made so proud
> That they have overborne their continents.

Notice how the text has a regular metrical form and a musical pulse, but does not rhyme. This is blank verse.

Let's compare this to Shakespeare's rhymed text, again in an example from *A Midsummer Night's Dream*. This time, the text is spoken by the character Helena as she laments the fact that her love, Demetrius, has fallen for her friend Hermia instead of for her. Here is a portion of her monologue:

> How happy some o'er other some can be!
> Through Athens I am thought as fair as she.
> But what of that? Demetrius thinks not so;
> He will not know what all but he do know:
> And as he errs, doting on Hermia's eyes,
> So I, admiring of his qualities.
> Things base and vile, holding no quantity,
> Love can transpose to form and dignity.
> Love looks not with the eyes, but with the mind;
> And therefore is wing'd Cupid painted blind:
> Nor hath Love's mind of any judgement taste;
> Wings and no eyes figure unheedy haste;
> And therefore is Love said to be a child,
> Because in choice he is so oft beguil'd.
> As waggish boys in game themselves forswear,
> So the boy Love is perjured every where;
> For ere Demetrius look'd on Hermia's eyne,
> He hail'd down oaths that he was only mine;
> And when this hail some heat from Hermia felt,
> So he dissolv'd, and showers of oaths did melt.

This verse has a regular pulse to it, but also has rhyming lines. *This particular rhyme scheme is called rhymed couplets—two successive lines of verse of which the final words rhyme with another* (Schwartz 2015).

Shakespeare also wrote many blank-verse speeches that, at the very end, have rhymed couplets. The speech cranks along for many lines unrhymed and then has one or two rhymed couplets at the very end. This makes for a snazzy little pop at the end of a speech. There are no clear examples of it in *A Midsummer Night's Dream* (the play where my other examples are from), so let's look at a nice little piece of text from *Twelfth Night*.

In this piece, Viola, disguised as a boy page named Cesario, is sent to deliver a message from her master to the grieving Lady Olivia. Viola is horrified to realize that Olivia, taken in by her disguise, may be developing a crush on her:

> I left no ring with her. What means this lady?
> Fortune forbid my outside have not charm'd her!
> She made good view of me; indeed so much
> That methought her eyes had lost her tongue,
> For she did speak in starts distractedly.
> She loves me sure, the cunning of her passion
> Invites me in this churlish messenger.
> None of my lord's ring! Why, he sent her none.
> I am the man! If it be so, as 'tis,
> Poor lady, she were better love a dream.
> Disguise, I see, thou art a wickedness,
> Wherein the pregnant enemy does much.
> How easy is it for the proper-false
> In women's waxen hearts to set their forms!
> Alas, [our] frailty is the cause, not we,
> For such as we are made [of], such we be.
> How will this fadge? my master loves her dearly,
> And I, (poor monster) fond as much on him;
> And she (mistaken) seems to dote on me.
> What will become of this? As I am man,
> My state is desperate for my master's love;
> As I am woman (now alas the day!),
> What thriftless sighs shall poor Olivia breathe!
> O time, thou must untangle this, not I,
> It is too hard a knot for me t' untie.

You can see that the speech is primarily blank verse until the last two lines, which end on the rhyme "I" and "untie."

This is a fairly common poetic device in Shakespeare's work, and he used it so often for a bunch of reasons. For one, the nice little rhyming ping at the end of the line tells the audience that something on stage just changed. The character is finished with something and is moving on to something else. They may simply be about to exit (remember, there was no stage lighting in Shakespeare's time, so in lieu of lighting cues, Shakespeare could employ poetic effects to signify a change of scene). The rhymed couplet could also signify that the character just had a major epiphany about something.

In the case above, Viola, throughout the body of the speech, is trying to figure out just what the heck is going on and if Olivia is really falling in love with her disguise as Cesario. At the end, on the rhymed couplet, she concludes that this problem is too difficult for her to solve, and that since she can't figure a way out of this mess, she'd better turn it over to a higher power. The rhymed couplet signifies both a mental conclusion and a physical exit.

Whatever the case, seeing a rhymed couplet at the end of a blank-verse speech is a signal to you, the actor, that you need to hit those juicy rhymes at the end. Shakespeare is expecting you to zazz things up, bringing that portion of the action on stage to a compelling close. (And how nice to end your audition speech on a little ping! Your words ring in the air. Weren't you terrific?)

Now let's step away from verse for a minute, even though it's so much fun. Here's an example of Shakespeare's prose, again from *Midsummer*, this time spoken by Bottom the Weaver. Ignorant, puffed-up Bottom has been under Fairy King Oberon's spell (Oberon's fairy henchman turned him into as ass!!). The spell is lifted, Bottom wakes up, and he recalls the recent events, which he regards as a dream.

> [Awaking] When my cue comes, call me, and I will answer: my next is, "Most fair Pyra-mus." Heigh-ho! Peter Quince! Flute, the bellows-mender! Snout, the tinker! Starveling! God's my life, stolen hence, and left me asleep! I have had a most rare vision. I have had a dream, past the wit of man to say what dream it was: man is but an ass, if he go about to expound this dream. Methought I was—there is no man can tell what. Methought I was,—and methought I had—but man is but [a patch'd]fool, if he will offer to say what methought I had. The eye of man hath not heard, the ear of man hath not seen, man's hand is not able to taste, his tongue to conceive, nor his heart to report, what my dream was. I will get Peter Quince to write a ballad of this dream: it shall be called "Bot-tom's Dream," because it hath no bottom; and I will sing it in the latter end of a play, before the Duke.Peradventure, to make it the more gracious, I shallsing it at her death. [Exit].

Now, a good Shakespeare editor (and we'll talk more about what I mean by "a good Shakespeare editor" in a minute) makes your job easy. He or she visually *shows* you what is prose and what is poetry by the way it is laid out on the page.

Compare the prose text for Bottom visually to the verse text for Helena and Titania in the same play, or the text for Viola from *Twelfth Night*. Do you see how the prose text looks like a regular old block like you'd find in any old book, while the poetry visually looks different on the page? This visual tells you everything you need to know! The pretty text is poetry. The blocky, regular-looking text is prose. It couldn't be easier to figure out, could it?

But you're an actor. Why am I bothering you with all of this? What do you care about the difference between poetry and prose? You have an audition coming up. This isn't English class.

My goal is to get you ready for that audition. And to get you ready for your audition, it's important for you, as an actor, to know what is verse and what isn't! When people request a classical piece for an audition, I think it's always a great idea to choose verse text (either blank or rhyming). Why? Well, nine times out of ten, that is what the people auditioning you are hoping to see.

If you do a verse piece, it will show that you can handle the requirements of speaking verse. In short, it will show that, if cast, you can handle the job of doing Shakespeare! It can also give the people auditioning you more information about your acting chops and your vocal and physical instrument than a prose piece. As someone who auditions actors, I can very quickly understand the quality of an actor's voice when they perform verse—it's just a little more athletic than prose.

The only exception that I would make to this rule (the Please-do-Verse-When-They-Ask-for-a-Classical-Piece rule) is this: if you are just an absolute lock for a predominantly prose role in a Shakespeare play, then and only then could you consider doing prose. Let's say, for instance, that you're a big, burly, quirky, funny guy and you're just perfect for a big, burly, quirky, funny role (for example, the Porter in *Macbeth*, who is the play's comic relief and speaks in prose). If you knew that the theatre was casting this role in *Macbeth* and you knew that you were just a perfect fit for it, you could bring in a Bottom piece from *Midsummer* in prose to audition with (side note: it's always a good idea not to use a piece from the show you are auditioning for, but to use a similar piece that helps the casting director to see you in that role). This is the one rare exception in my mind. Otherwise, people really want to see some verse text—so give the people what they want! Some snazzy, sexy verse text.

3. Your Friend, the Editor, and Other Great Helpers

A good Shakespeare editor is your new best friend. Not all Shakespeare editions are created equal. If I want to get myself a copy of *The Grapes of Wrath* to read, pretty much any copy of *The Grapes of Wrath* is going to be the same. If I want to get a volume of Robert Frost's poetry, any edition will have pretty much the same content. Not so with Shakespeare.

There is no one definitive version of Shakespeare's writing. Why? Because Mr. Shakespeare wrote his work to be performed live rather than read. Since plays were meant to be performed and not published in Shakespeare's time, it not only was unnecessary to create written versions of the plays, it could also be detrimental to profits! If the play were written down, a competing theatre company could have stolen it and presented the work in their theatre. Sometimes unscrupulous publishers bought copies of the plays from equally unscrupulous actors who had recalled the play from memory or had obtained a handwritten copy. As Michael J. Cummings (2003) explains, "These methods of acquiring a copy [of the play] often resulted in the publication of scripts with many errors. To preserve the integrity of a play, the acting company that owned the script sometimes made its own arrangements to publish the text. Consequently, different printed versions of the play—some accurate, some inaccurate—were in circulation."

My colleague, Shakespeare scholar Bruce Avery, explains further:

> For many of Shakespeare's plays there is more than one original text behind the modern copy you hold in your hand. During his life, those plays of Shakespeare that made it into print emerged as "Quartos," small, cheap, and often badly printed single editions of plays such as *Romeo and Juliet* and *Hamlet*. As far as we know Shakespeare had no interest in, nor editorial control over, these texts. Seven years after his death, however, Shakespeare's friends and theater partners John Heminge and William Condell collected all of his existing plays into an impressively printed and bound Complete Works, usually referred as the First Folio. In those plays printed in both Quarto and Folio, there are often numerous and significant differences.

Because we cannot trust that any one particular written account of Shakespeare's plays are truly the exact version Shakespeare gave to his actors, there is ambiguity. This is where the editor matters to you the actor. And this is why a good editor is your new best friend.

> A Shakespeare editor's task is especially laborious because, since there is no authoritative manuscript behind a play, he or she has to choose among various intermediary sources, each with its own strengths and weaknesses. An editor's decisions have an enormous effect on the text we read, its meaning, sound, and sense. For instance, where Shakespeare left punctuation ambiguous, it's up to the editor to choose: did Shakespeare intend "No!," "no?", or "No?" Should a word be on a line by itself or should it start a new one? (Epstein 1993).

Look at the above example; "No!," "no?", or "No?" If you are an English literature major who is reading the text, these variously edited "nos" are different and possibly a bit interesting but are not necessarily game-changers. But if you are *acting* the text, these little subtle differences equate to big, honking differences in your performance. "No!" as an emphatic declaration is drastically different that small, lowercase "no?" as a tentative, pondering question. This is but one small example of a text and punctuation choice made by an editor that has big ramifications in your world as the actor.

You see, Shakespeare editors have enormous power over meaning, not only in a small sense (like punctuation and word choices), but in an even larger sense. Would you believe that there is a whole speech in Hamlet that is up for debate among editors? Various Shakespearean editors cannot agree whether to include Hamlet's soliloquy in Act 4, scene 4, "How all occasions do inform against me," in the play. The soliloquy appears in the Second Quarto (Q2) version of the text but does not appear in the First Folio. The decision by an editor to include or exclude this soliloquy changes Hamlet's journey and ultimate destination as a character.

Given that these editorial choices can greatly affect meaning, you can see how having a great Shakespeare editor by your side will help you do your best work as an actor. Their editorial choices translate directly into your performance.

There are so many versions of Shakespeare's texts out there that I can't possibly advocate for or caution against all of your options, but I can tell you a general no-no and suggest a few great sources as you begin your hunt for texts.

Laura's big no-no: don't pull a text from the Internet. Although there are a few excellent sources out there, there are some that aren't reliably edited. Internet Shakespeare sources, for the most part, are too sketchy to be trusted. Even a good Internet source (like the MIT web version, which is fairly faithfully edited) doesn't show you a wonderfully clear page layout (like the printed sources I'm about to suggest). Deciphering poetry from prose is trickier online, whereas with a great text edition in front of you, it is crystal-clear. Many online versions also aren't well punctuated. Good printed editions, in general, are just clearer to work from as an actor.

Here's an example. Once upon a time, my student brought this monologue into class to work on for an upcoming audition. It is Macbeth's monologue when he is about to kill the King. This is the text version my student found on the Internet:

> If it were done when 'tis done, then 'twere well
> It were done quickly: if the assassination
> Could trammel up the consequence, and catch
> With his surcease success; that but this blow
> Might be the be-all and the end-all here,
> But here, upon this bank and shoal of time,
> We'ld jump the life to come. (Hylton 1993)

Well, my poor student (one of my brighter and more talented students, mind you) couldn't really make any sensible acting choices with the piece. He was especially stumped on what to do with the "his surcease success" part. It was just a big bunch of mush. Then I pulled out my faithful *Riverside Shakespeare* and saw that the text was punctuated in a way that made a whole lot more sense:

> If it were done, when 'tis done, then 'twere well
> It were done quickly. If th' assassination
> Could trammel up the consequence, and catch
> With his surcease, success; that but this blow
> Might be the be-all and the end-all—here,
> But here, upon this bank and [shoal] of time,
> We'ld jump the life to come.

You can see that a well-punctuated text does a lot of the acting work for you. In addition to having some extra commas in the first line of text that help the actor make sense of things, the punctuation in the second and third lines is a *huge* help. In this second version we have a separation between the words "surcease" and "success." In the Internet text they are treated as a single entity: "surcease success." What is "surcease success"? It makes no sense. In the nicely edited version from *The Riverside*, the words being separated with punctuation helps us to understand that Macbeth means, "and with his death (his surcease), I will have success!"

When you are acting a text, little things make a big, big difference.

Here are a few truly great texts to get you started:

- *The Oxford Shakespeare: The Complete Works,* Stanley Wells, Gary Taylor, John Jowett, William Montgomery
- *The Arden Shakespeare Complete Works*, Ann Thompson, David Scott Kastanm Richard Proudfoot
- *The Complete Works of Shakespeare,* David Bevington
- *The Riverside Shakespeare*, G. Blakemore Evans, J. J. M. Tobin

Different editions of each version are available. For our purposes, any edition will do, and older editions may come cheaper for you. Used volumes by these editors are often available online or in used bookstores, so don't feel like you have to drop a bundle of cash to get a wonderful version. You'll be very happy that you made the purchase.

What do I love about these four versions? They're beautifully edited by some of the world's most renowned Shakespeare scholars. They're clear to look at, and most of these editions (not all printings) have nice footnotes to get you started. After many years teaching Shakespeare, I can say that these are my favorites. I do not walk into a classroom without all four these days. Why do I bring four different versions to class, you might ask? Why not just bring one well-edited version with me? I bring all four so that my actors can follow along and compare the different editors' choices, like word variations and punctuation differences, to come up with a version of the text that we find the most electric. It actually becomes an incredibly fun game. Every time I do this, I make a new discovery with my students.

In addition to good editions (that's a mouthful), let's talk about the other great resources that would be terrific to have at your disposal as you work on your piece.

You need some good Shakespeare word guides! These fall under two categories:

- Pronouncing the words
- Understanding the meaning of the words

There are lots of terrific resources out there, and as technology booms, more and more resources are becoming available on your phone or tablet than I can even keep track of. But you can't go wrong with these great choices:

For pronouncing the words, here is my favorite guide, called, rather simply, *Pronouncing Shakespeare's Words* by Dale Coye. This guide lists the most common words in Shakespeare that you'll need to pronounce in your piece, with a phonetic guide to help you out. It breaks things down play by play, helping you to pronounce both the character names in that play and the words in the play that you're most likely to have questions about. Borrow it from the library if you don't want to invest right now, but you really need to say those character names and words correctly at your audition. A mispronounced character name, place name, mythological reference, or archaic word can grate on the ear of the person auditioning you! Here's a great and easy way to make sure that you get it right in your audition.

To look up word meanings, and the meanings of archaic references, there are many options. Many Shakespeare editions often have some helpful footnotes included. These can get you started, but they're not always enough to really unpack the meaning of some sticky places in your piece. Here are my two favorites:

- *Shakespeare's Words: A Glossary and Language Companion*, David Crystal and Ben Crystal
- *A Shakespeare Glossary*, C. T. Onions and Robert D. Eagleson

Another great resource is the *Shakespeare Lexicon and Quotation Dictionary* by Alexander Schmidt. Though not quite as portable as the other two language glossaries, it is incredibly comprehensive. You may also want to check out the brief online guide at Shakespeare's Words. Look at the Frequently Encountered Words section: shakespearewords.com/FEW.

Why do you need this? Because it isn't enough to just get the gist of what you are saying on stage. The more you really, truly, deeply understand what you, as the character, are saying, the more confidently you own the piece. It's amazing how a general understanding of what you're saying leads to a general performance. A specific, nuanced understanding of the words you're speaking translates into clear and compelling acting choices. When you see some murky performance of Shakespeare on-stage, my bet is that the actor understands the surface meaning of what he is saying, but not the nitty-gritty heart of it. Ever see Kenneth Branagh, Sir Ian McKellen, or Dame Judi Dench perform Shakespeare? You can bet that they know every single word they're speaking.

You don't need to be a Shakespeare scholar to do that too. You just need to have a good Shakespeare scholar or two on your table to do all of the hard work for you. With the right tools—like the sources that I just suggested to you—it's a piece of cake.

4. What Makes a Great Classical Audition?

I cringe to think about my early Shakespeare auditions.

I was terrible. Truly. And I was terrible not because I was a bad actor, but because I chose the wrong material.

The reason that I chose the wrong material was twofold:

- I didn't really *know* Shakespeare's plays. I didn't know how to find the right piece in this overwhelming canon of work. I didn't know how to do any kind of intelligent or skilled search for something that was right, so I just settled on what I could find easily.
- I didn't really know what people were expecting of me. I didn't understand what made a good audition piece and what didn't. (I mean, it was all Shakespeare, right? So therefore it was all equally good . . .)

I wonder if you're in the same fog now that I was in then. So let's see if I can help you.

What are people looking for when you do a Shakespeare piece? I certainly can't answer for everybody, but I can answer for myself.

A "good" Shakespeare piece is, in short, one that you think is great fun to do. That's my number-one criterion. If it isn't fun and juicy and exciting, why do it? That was my big problem years ago. I wasn't jazzed about my pieces. I was ho-hum about them. With all of that amazing material, why settle for feeling ho-hum? Find something great! So, when you read potential pieces, try them on like you would items of clothing. Does this fit well? Do you love saying these words? Are you excited to be this person? I guarantee that if you skim through enough plays, you'll find a piece you feel this way about—and when you find it, you'll know it.

A "good" Shakespeare piece also shows the auditioners something about who you are. It can show your intelligence, playfulness, sense of fun, intensity, sensuality, dangerousness, vulnerability—and in an ideal world it can show many of these qualities all at once. Shakespeare packs a lot of action and tactical shifts into a short amount of time, so you can take your auditioner/audience on quite a journey very quickly. But to do this, you have to feel an affinity for the piece.

Now is not a good time to "stretch" yourself. I have a musical theatre student who is a kick-butt soprano. She can sing a *Light in the Piazza* that will make you weep within thirty seconds from its sheer lyrical beauty. I once coached her for an upcoming audition and she brought in a belt alto piece from Sondheim's *Follies*. "Why did you choose this piece for your audition?" I asked her. "I wanted to stretch myself and show my range," she told me. As noble as this idea was, the piece wasn't *her*. It was the wrong age, the wrong type, the wrong everything.

Acting class is where you "stretch" yourself. Auditions are where you choose what lies well within your reach. That doesn't mean for a minute that you don't take risks as an actor, but it means that you should take risks with your acting choices, not with your choice of material. What do I mean by this? If you are twenty-two years old, now is not the time to be King Lear. Do what you can connect to easily. That doesn't mean you won't have work to do to master your piece, but at least you will be meeting the text for the first time as a relatable friend and not as a foreigner.

Don't worry too terribly much about overdone pieces. "Overdone" Shakespeare pieces are overdone because they are so darn good. There's also no way to really know what's being overdone at any given time. A few years ago I sat graduate auditions for an MFA program that I worked at. I was astounded that more than half of the actors I saw that year brought in pieces from *King John*, *Pericles*, and *Titus Andronicus*. I'm sure the actors' line of thinking was something like this: "Well, no one does *King John*! I'll look for an audition piece from *King John*! I'll be the only one doing it! Go me." Yup. Except for the other one hundred and fifty actors who had the exact same thought; so many people knew that no one does *King John* that that year everybody was doing *King John!* While it's always preferable to choose a novel audition piece that others aren't doing, you really have no way of knowing who's doing what. Yes, there are a few pieces that have been done to death at certain points in time, but pieces go in and out of vogue. Honestly, others may feel differently, but for me, a beautifully done Shakespeare piece never loses its magic.

A great audition for me is also one where you let the text do all of the work for you. Later on we'll talk more about that, but it's worth putting that idea into your head as we turn toward selecting your piece. Do you know how on those What-Not-to-Wear shows the makeover person says harsh things to the poor makeover-ee, like, "Were you wearing that dress, or was that dress wearing *you*?" (ooh, snap) It's kind of the same thing with your Shakespeare piece. When you simply embrace the right text, you don't need to generate much. The action is in the word. Speak the words with clarity, understanding, and commitment, with a focus on changing the person that you are talking to, and you wear the poetry like a tailor-made suit. Force physicality, layer on cluttered, extraneous physical action or disconnected vocal choices, and all of a sudden you're wearing a clunky, shapeless acting muumuu. Shakespeare is all in the words, and the words are all you need; so choose the words well and wisely.

5. Finding Your Match

by Stephanie Ann Foster

You've got your great Shakespeare edition from your skilled editor. Check.

You've got your pronunciation guide to help you properly pronounce the words.

Check.

You've got your language guide to uncover nuanced meaning and archaic words.

Check.

Okay, now what?

Now we start to find your match.

In order to do that, it will be helpful to get a better understanding of the categories of plays that Shakespeare wrote. Once you understand this, it will be even easier to narrow down what kinds of pieces might be right for you.

In this chapter you'll learn how to . . .

- Understand the play categories (and get helpful hints for handling them)
- Consider the gender, age, and status that you want to play
- Choose three to five characters that most appeal to you

THE PLAY CATEGORIES

Shakespeare's plays fall into several categories, and performers are sometimes surprised to learn that those categories extend beyond the traditional "comedy and tragedy" headings, and that not even the upper echelons of academia have come to a conclusive decision about how to divide the plays. It's important to know where your chosen play falls in the canon, however, because each category (no matter how debated) carries with it a stylistic history that might inform the opinions of those watching. Here are the basic types of plays, and some helpful tips for approaching them.

Comedies

Though they often include flashes of pathos, these plays are primarily intended to make people laugh or jubilate. They close with weddings and celebrations—with couples reunited and losses restored. The Shakespeare comedies include *As You Like It*, *The Comedy of Errors*, *Love's Labour's Lost*,

The Merry Wives of Windsor, A Midsummer Night's Dream, Much Ado about Nothing, The Taming of the Shrew, The Two Gentlemen of Verona, The Two Noble Kinsmen, and *Twelfth Night.*

Tip for Comedies

Take yourself seriously. Though they make irrational decisions and are faced with ridiculous situations, the humor of these characters springs from the fact that they really mean everything they say. Helena of *A Midsummer Night's Dream* is genuine when she begs her former lover Demetrius to *use her like a dog.* Sir Toby Belch of *Twelfth Night* really means it when he compares the girl of his dreams to a *beagle.* Dromio in *The Comedy of Errors* is in earnest when he refers to himself as *an ass and a woman's man*—that's why it's funny. Much like the way babies make us laugh by responding to everyday occurrences as if they were tragedies, Shakespeare's comedic characters make us laugh because they take the ridiculous things that happen to them so very seriously.

If you have read some of the plays mentioned above, then the first thing you might have noticed about the comedies is that, well, they aren't always *funny.* Modern audiences often pity *Twelfth Night's* Malvolio when he is tossed into a dark room and tormented by his captors. Most readers find the treatment of the Jew Shylock downright cruel and anti-Semitic. This leads us to a second category that some scholars use to further divide the Shakespeare comedies.

The Problem Plays, Dark Comedies, or Tragicomedies

These plays not only pose a "problem" for readers that try to categorize them, they also each have a central problem posed by the playwright—often a problem faced by society at large, such as "Can justice to one be served by injustice to another?" or "Is virtue more valuable than life?" These plays seem to vacillate between extreme light and dark, often shifting so suddenly between the two that modern audiences struggle to keep up. Are we really supposed to celebrate when we've just seen so much darkness? Academics argue over which plays to include in this category, but the major contenders are: *All's Well That Ends Well, Measure for Measure, Troilus and Cressida, The Winter's Tale, Timon of Athens, The Two Noble Kinsmen,* and *The Merchant of Venice.*

Tip for Problem Plays or Dark Comedies

The problem with this category is that it is difficult to know how each director plans to approach the play (honoring more of its comedy or more of its tragedy). That's the same question you'll need to answer as an actor. Have you chosen this piece as your more dramatic offering, or as your comedic one? Both options are acceptable because, more than any of the other plays, the dark comedies are up for reinterpretation. Directors and actors often embark on bold interpretive journeys with these scripts. You want to try Portia from *The Merchant of Venice* as a tragic figure? Go for it. You want to make Antonio a smiling fool who doesn't realize the trap he blunders into with a debt collector? Give it a try. There are, however, two hot-button characters to be wary of: Kate and Shylock. As the primary representatives of their types within the texts (a strong, opinionated female who does not wish to marry, and a Jew who participates in moneylending), these two characters are usually handled with care and played somewhat sympathetically in order to avoid misrepresenting an entire people group (all women, or all Jews). If you fail to do so, you run the risk of making your audition about politics rather than skill.

Tragedies

These are the plays that actors are most likely to have studied in depth. Preferred by educational institutions because their content hinges on universal human emotions and meaningful themes, the tragedies center on noble-born or high-status protagonists who suffer for their fatal flaws. These include *Titus Andronicus, Romeo and Juliet, Julius Caesar, Hamlet, Troilus and Cressida, Othello, King Lear, Macbeth, Timon of Athens, Antony and Cleopatra, Coriolanus*, and *Cymbeline*.

Tip for Tragedies

Know your flaw. Play it, and play the opposite. Every character in a tragedy has one key trait that will lead to their destruction, and that flaw is present from the beginning. It is present, at least in part, in every monologue. It is what drives your character, even if he or she is not always aware of it. Find your flaw and you have found your monologue's engine. Once you've found your flaw, remember not only to play it, but to also play *against* it. Most characters find themselves struggling against their flaws (Romeo's boyish love turned to hate, Juliet's passion for life turned to desire for death, Hamlet's indecision turned to rash action). The old acting adage "play the opposite" is especially true in tragedy. Whatever your key character's defining quality might be, remember that he or she is also fighting *against* that trait. This struggle can inform and deepen your experience with your chosen monologue.

"Wait!" I hear you saying, "Some of the plays you listed just now sound like histories!" That is very true (and congratulations if you caught that). However, as far as most modern scholarship is concerned, when we speak of the Shakespeare histories, we're really only talking about the *English* histories (sorry, Rome, Egypt, Scotland, and ancient Britain—you don't count).

Histories

The histories include the rarely produced plays *King John* and *Henry VIII*, and they also include the eight plays covering the history and pre-history of the Wars of the Roses. You'll notice that it is often "wars" in the plural and not "war" in the singular. This is because the history of this conflict stretched across several major battles and monarchies, eventually becoming a central part of English history and identity. Here's a brief historical recap:

THE WARS OF THE ROSES (1455–1485) AT A GLANCE

Richard II deposed by cousin Henry IV (1399)

Factions form over the next generations.
Who should rule?
(All major contenders are Plantagenet.)

The House of Plantagenet splits:

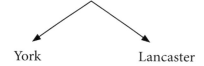

York   Lancaster

Symbol: white rose		Symbol: red rose
French supporters	defeated by	Henry V
		(Battle of Agincourt/St. Crispin's)
Richard III	killed by	Henry VII (Battle of Bosworth Field
Elizabeth of York	marries	Henry VII (Henry *Tudor*)

The two sides have now united!
We have a new ruling house:

The Tudors!

We also have a new symbol: the Tudor rose is both red *and* white.

The histories are often further divided into two *tetralogies* (use this word if you want to sound impressive):

The First Tetralogy:	The Second Tetralogy (The "Henriad"):
Henry VI, Part 1	Richard II
Henry VI, Part 2	Henry IV, Part 1
Henry VI, Part 3	Henry IV, Part 2
Richard III	Henry V

You might have noted that the kings in the first tetralogy seem to come *after* the kings in the second tetralogy (after all, shouldn't *Richard II* come before *Richard III*?). This is because an important aspect of Shakespeare scholarship has been to determine *chronology of composition*. It's a lot like the *Star Wars* franchise—the later episodes of the story were actually written first. However, if you want to watch or understand all of the plays in order, you have to start with the second tetralogy, just like if you want to have the whole *Star Wars* experience in order you have to start with *Star Wars Episode One: The Phantom Menace*, even though it wasn't made first. Make sense?

Tip for Histories

Know your history. Just kidding—you don't have to know all of it. No one in the audition room expects you to be a history scholar, but there will likely be references in your monologue to past conflicts or political betrayals, and it is important that you understand the significance of those events in order for your monologue to feel rooted.

For example, here is one aspect of the history plays that sometimes escapes modern actors: *kingship matters*. The crown *matters*. Regardless of which character you have chosen, if he or she is from a history play, then he or she has a deep investment in who wears the crown of England. He or she has lost relatives and friends to that bloody conflict. When you speak of the crown, the throne, a king's authority, or a king's anointing, you are speaking of something very near to your heart. Too often, when I hear new performers speak of kingship, they sound the way we might sound when we speak of political parties today—detached, slightly agitated, but ultimately safe from harm. When it comes to kingship, no one is safe from harm. (We'll talk more about how to get a handle on the histories a little bit later.)

The Romances or Late Romances

The First Folio—the seminal edition of the plays, first published in 1623 by two of Shakespeare's surviving contemporaries—does not include a "romance" category. However, modern scholars (and actors) must be aware of this category, and it offers a very helpful place to store those pesky (and beautiful) final Shakespeare plays. They include: *Pericles, Prince of Tyre; Cymbeline; The Winter's Tale; The Tempest;* and (sometimes) *The Two Noble Kinsmen.* Likely written at the end of Shakespeare's career, these plays are called "romances" not because they depict romantic love, but because they resemble the medieval romances that often included magical elements and vast spans of time and place. The plays contain whole countries, empires, and other worlds. They include magic, the intervention of the gods, and harrowing journeys that culminate in reunions sad and blessed. They are considered by many to be the most complex and the most beautiful of the Shakespeare canon.

Tip for Romances

In these plays you have *great flexibility of characterization.* For example, we do not know what Ceres, goddess of grain, sounds like. Perhaps she is ethereal, with a voice like golden sunbeams, or perhaps she is deep-voiced and as earthy as her crops; the performer has total freedom to make this character unique. These are not historical characters bound by the events of the past. Their magic often transcends time, meaning that we can have a very ancient fairy servant Ariel, if we wish. We can also have a young goddess Juno, played by an impetuous teen, if we like. This is also the category of plays in which gender typically has the least sway on casting decisions. In the 2010 film adaptation of *The Tempest,* for example, the ancient sorcerer and father Prospero was played (to critical acclaim) by Helen Mirren. I recently sat in on a beautiful audition in which a young man played the part of Miranda. That kind of playful experimentation is often welcomed in the romances, which have fewer entrenched audience expectations than widely popular classics like *Romeo and Juliet.* The romances are arguably the most imaginative of the plays—they practically beg to be reimagined by each director and actor.

THREE FACTORS TO CONSIDER: GENDER, AGE, AND STATUS

There are three basics to consider when choosing a character: gender, age, and social status.

Happily, gender is quickly becoming a more flexible factor in casting Shakespeare's plays. There have been female versions of all the great male characters, and men have been cast in the roles of Shakespeare's women since the plays were first produced. However, it is important to know the original intended gender of your character. It isn't always what you might think based on the character's name. For example, "Dorcas" and "Charmian"? Women. "Florizel" and "Dolabella"? Men.

It is also important to know the basic age range of your character. Shakespeare does not always provide us with character ages, but he does give us helpful clues with the words "aged" and "youth." It can be difficult for an actor to answer the questions "Is this role too old for me? Can I pull this off?" The chart below should help you to decide if a character falls into the correct age range for you. Keep in mind that age range is typically much more flexible in an educational setting.

Lastly, and perhaps most importantly, you must consider *status*. It's status that tells you how your character relates to the other people in the play, how your character behaves physically, and how he or she expects to be perceived. There are two kinds of status:

Status by Birth

This is where your character falls within the range of Elizabethan/Jacobean society. For example, some scholars arrange the status of the period in the following order:

monarch
nobles
merchants
tradesmen
laborers

Relative Status

This is how your character compares to the others around them. For example, there are several "gentlemen" and "sirs" in the plays who never appear on stage with anyone of lower status than themselves. They often function as the letter carriers and news bringers and have very little power. If you are playing one of these characters, you need to bear in mind that, while your character was born to manners and wealth, he or she may be speaking to characters of much higher status.

Similarly, some characters deserve high status but simply aren't granted it. The captains Fluellen, Macmorris, and Jamy (of *Henry V*) are all advanced military leaders. However, because they are also Welsh, Irish, and Scottish, these three are never quite granted the respect of their English military counterparts in the other plays.

The tried-and-true method for determining basic status is to look at the style of writing Shakespeare used. In general: prose is low-status and verse is high-status. Although there are exceptions to this scheme (even characters like Hamlet flip into prose now and then), this is definitely a trick worth knowing. That said, it doesn't help you to know that a character has a high-status birth if you don't also know that the character is basically only a glorified messenger or servant; that's where relative status comes in handy. For the chart that follows, we've given slight priority to relative status. You'll see a few lords and sirs included among the low-status characters because that's how they function in the play.

What's the Difference?

Characters with high relative status are often masters of PR. They must consider manners and how to maintain their position with strict adherence to courtly norms, or with blatant shows of power. Characters with low relative status must consider how to appease authority figures. However, they are also generally freer to behave outside of social norms.

Though flexibility is the hallmark of a strong actor, most performers show a penchant for either high-status or low-status characters—which one is your strength? Which would you find most fun to play?

FINDING THE ONE FOR YOU!

Now it is time to find a character that is a match for the age, type, and status level you want to play. Several of these ranges and types are presented here, along with a brief description of each character—to help pique your interest.

These categories are not hard-and-fast. For example, who is to say that "Clown" is a male rather than a female? We leave gender bending up to you the actor, and have presented here what was likely the original intended gender, age, and relative status of each character, based on context clues.

To further assist you, we've included only characters with enough lines to feasibly make up an audition monologue (albeit in some cases a very short one)—at least six strong lines. We've also included a character if we see a strong potential for some of his or her lines to be woven together into a strong monologue.

We suggest that you read the short descriptions below and mark the five character descriptions that most appeal to you. Look for descriptions that resonate with you or spark your creativity.

YOUNGER TO MIDDLE-AGED MEN (HIGH STATUS)

Bertram	*All's Well That Ends Well*	(handsome but detached cad)
Parolles	*All's Well That Ends Well*	(disloyal poser full of lies)
First Lord Dumaine	*All's Well That Ends Well*	(clever exposer of disloyal poser)
Second Lord Dumaine	*All's Well That Ends Well*	(clever exposer of disloyal poser)
Orlando	*As You Like It*	(manly, neglected, heart-of-gold)

Oliver	*As You Like It*	(jealous bully big brother)
First Lord	*As You Like It*	(mocker of melancholy Jaques)
Jacques de Boys (Son)	*As You Like It*	(reporter of good tidings; risks life)
Le Beau	*As You Like It*	(gossipy courtier; likes wrestlers)
King Ferdinand	*Love's Labour's Lost*	(zealous scholar; shuns women)
Berowne/Biron	*Love's Labour's Lost*	(outspoken thoughtful flirter)
Longaville	*Love's Labour's Lost*	(love-struck love-letter writer)
Dumain	*Love's Labour's Lost*	(moony bad love-poem writer)
Lucio	*Measure for Measure*	(flamboyant playboy; "a fantastic")
Claudio	*Measure for Measure*	(desperate hot-head on death row)
Bassanio	*The Merchant of Venice*	(lover boy borrows; risks friend)
Gratiano	*The Merchant of Venice*	(coarse friend; hurls insults; loves)
Lorenzo	*The Merchant of Venice*	(has a secret love; elopes with Jew)
Prince of Arragon	*The Merchant of Venice*	(arrogant Spaniard; rejected)
Prince of Morocco	*The Merchant of Venice*	(foreigner; flatterer; rejected)
Fenton	*The Merry Wives of Windsor*	(highborn; broke; falls for rich gal)
Slender	*The Merry Wives of Windsor*	(incompetent coward; wooing fop)
Demetrius	*A Midsummer Night's Dream*	(arrogant playboy shuns ex gal)
Lysander	*A Midsummer Night's Dream*	(true lover; made untrue by magic)
Claudio	*Much Ado about Nothing*	(hasty hot-blooded soldier; loves)
Lucentio	*The Taming of the Shrew*	(romantic; stars in eyes; bold)
Ferdinand	*The Tempest*	(romantic prince; chivalrous)
Sebastian	*The Tempest*	(gullible betrayer of brother)
Proteus	*The Two Gentlemen of Verona*	(mercurial flirtatious cheater)
Valentine	*The Two Gentlemen of Verona*	(banished lover; forest king; true)
Sebastian	*Twelfth Night*	(mourning sister; bold; romantic)
First Gentleman	*The Winter's Tale*	(witnesses great and pitiable acts)
Florizel	*The Winter's Tale*	(disguised prince in love; brave)
Gentleman	*The Winter's Tale*	(eloquent; admires virtue/beauty)
Mark Antony	*Antony and Cleopatra*	(torn between duty and passion)
Pompey	*Antony and Cleopatra*	(ambitious; cunning threat)
Arviragus	*Cymbeline*	(poetic sensitive twin; disguised)
Cloten	*Cymbeline*	(forceful jerk; doesn't get the girl)
Guiderius	*Cymbeline*	(bold and active disguised prince)
Iachimo	*Cymbeline*	(villainous cad; gambler; peeper)
Hamlet	*Hamlet*	(indecisive brooder; possibly mad)
Fortinbras	*Hamlet*	(bold strategic war leader; heart)
Laertes	*Hamlet*	(protective bro; revenger; gallant)
Mark Antony	*Julius Caesar*	(grieves; politically machinates)

(Marcus) Brutus	*Julius Caesar*	(honorable idealist; kills; suicide)
Cassius	*Julius Caesar*	(manipulator; lean and hungry)
Octavius Caesar	*Julius Caesar*	(future emperor; sword drawn)
Edgar	*King Lear*	(future king; disguiser; hero; true)
Malcolm	*Macbeth*	(true king; wily and wise; hero)
Gratiano	*Othello*	(chivalrous; defender of women)
Lodovico	*Othello*	(confronts attacker of women)
Benvolio	*Romeo and Juliet*	(pacifist; concerned cousin; good)
Mercutio	*Romeo and Juliet*	(mercurial; swordsman; madman)
Romeo	*Romeo and Juliet*	(brooding poet; lover; ill fate)
Tybalt	*Romeo and Juliet*	(hot-tempered swordsman; bold)
Bassianus	*Titus Andronicus*	(virtuous; princely; rescues love)
Chiron	*Titus Andronicus*	(violent youth; bored; lustful)
Demetrius	*Titus Andronicus*	(bloodthirsty; corrupt; smart)
Lucius	*Titus Andronicus*	(popular; warring; mourns losses)
Martius	*Titus Andronicus*	(finds brother dead; sorrowful)
Quintus	*Titus Andronicus*	(fearful; trembles; finds horror)
Young Lucius	*Titus Andronicus*	(emotional; reads adventures)
Achilles	*Troilus and Cressida*	(prideful thug; preening; bully)
Ajax	*Troilus and Cressida*	(cousin to princes; easily duped)
Hector	*Troilus and Cressida*	(mighty hero prince; admits flaws)
Paris	*Troilus and Cressida*	(prince; stole love; chivalrous)
Troilus	*Troilus and Cressida*	(true faithful lover; prince)
Earl of Douglas	*Henry IV, Part 1*	(brave warrior; honorable Scot)
King Henry V (Hal)	*Henry IV, Part 1*	(seeming rebel; honorable; smart)
King Henry V (Hal)	*Henry IV, Part 2*	(maturing; rejects bad-boy ways)
Hotspur	*Henry IV, Part 1*	(wild rebel; honor obsessed)
Prince John	*Henry IV, Part 2*	(leads; tricks enemies weaponless)
Louis the Dauphin	*Henry V*	(bold mocker; arrogant; ignores)
Charles, King of France	*Henry VI, Part 1*	(duelist; flirt; makes peace to save)
Earl of Salisbury	*Henry VI, Part 1*	(eager for battle; too eager; dies)
Earl of Suffolk	*Henry VI, Part 1*	(woos captured lady; influencer)
Earl of Warwick	*Henry VI, Part 1*	(acts as judge; highly moral; just)
King Henry VI	*Henry VI, Part 1*	(prophesied against; young; weds)
John Talbot	*Henry VI, Part 1*	(honorable to a fault; brave death)
Earl of Suffolk	*Henry VI, Part 2*	(in love with queen; conspires)
Earl of Warwick	*Henry VI, Part 2*	(supports the white rose; logical)
Henry VI	*Henry VI, Part 2*	(ineffectual; trades for wife; weak)
Richard the Younger	*Henry VI, Part 2*	(deformed; rapier wit; Richard III)

Young Clifford	*Henry VI, Part 2*	(swears to revenge father's death)
Duke of Somerset	*Henry VI, Part 3*	(vacillates; his heart misgives)
Edmond, Earl of Rutland	*Henry VI, Part 3*	(young boy fears murderer; dies)
George (of Clarence)	*Henry VI, Part 3*	(turncoat; coward; kills; spares)
Edward IV	*Henry VI, Part 3*	(seducer; speech-maker; murders)
Louis XI	*Henry VI, Part 3*	(punishes dishonor; wants peace)
Prince Edward	*Henry VI, Part 3*	(unrestrainable; arrogant; killed)
Richard III	*Henry VI, Part 3*	(deformed vile oath-breaker; lies)
Cromwell	*Henry VIII*	(protégé watches master's fall)
Earl of Surrey	*Henry VIII*	(seeks revenge; sees corruption)
Gardiner	*Henry VIII*	(snake; puts cardinal before king)
Sir Henry Guildford	*Henry VIII*	(master of ceremonies; happy)
Arthur	*King John*	(imprisoned; not at fault; just a boy)
First Gentleman	*Henry VIII*	(political enthusiast; shares news)
Third Gentleman	*Henry VIII*	(knows gossip; loathes masses)
Chatillion	*King John*	(failed mission; messenger; warns)
Robert Faulconbridge	*King John*	(thinks his brother is king's bastard; greedy)
Louis the Dauphin	King John	(backstabber; fiery; unscrupulous)
Earl of Pembroke	King John	(flip-flops; finally sides with England)
Philip the Bastard	King John	(son of Lionheart; bold; matures)
Prince Henry	King John	(honorable son; hopeful; forgives)
Earl of Salisbury	King John	(rebel leader; true honor; avenger)
First Lord	Pericles	(wants to find and serve a king)
Duke of Aumerle	Richard II	(scraping bumbler; saved by mom)
Earl of Northumberland	Richard II	(fights to depose king; no respect)
Earl of Salisbury	Richard II	(loyal; unable to save his king)
Henry IV	Richard II	(grieves dissolute son; takes over)
Lord Fitzwater	Richard II	(confident; wants to fight; fiery)
Sir Stephen Scroop	Richard II	(unhappy messenger of war)
Boy (Edward)	Richard III	(wise beyond his years; learning)
Duke of York (Boy)	Richard III	(concerned about growth; jests)
Duke of Clarence	Richard III	(imprisoned for prophecy/initials)
Marquis of Dorset	Richard III	(hated; wise enough to skip town)
Richard III	Richard III	(glee; wicked; revenge; lie; seduce)

MIDDLE-AGED TO OLDER MEN (HIGH STATUS)

King of France	*All's Well That Ends Well*	(grateful; admires miracle healer)
Lafeu/Lafew	*All's Well That Ends Well*	(wise advisor; sees through lies)
Duke Senior	*As You Like It*	(exiled; wisdom from nature; kind)

Jaques	*As You Like It*	(melancholic poetic observer)
Duke Frederick	*As You Like It*	(cruel usurper; violent temper)
Lord Amiens	*As You Like It*	(blithe companion songster)
First Lord	*As You Like It*	(mocker of melancholy Jaques)
Duke Solinus	*The Comedy of Errors*	(authoritative lawmaker; pardons)
Boyet	*Love's Labour's Lost*	(amused lord, serves princess)
Don Adriano de Armado	*Love's Labour's Lost*	("a fantastical Spaniard" — in lust)
Duke Vincentio	*Measure for Measure*	(kind ruler disguised as low friar)
Escalus	*Measure for Measure*	(wise lord; advises mercy; torn)
Angelo	*Measure for Measure*	(merciless hypocrite; entices nun)
Holofernes	*Love's Labour's Lost*	(pedantic schoolmaster babbler)
Sir Nathaniel	*Love's Labour's Lost*	(pedantic curate babbler)
Antonio	*The Merchant of Venice*	(merchant; risks flesh for friend)
Duke	*The Merchant of Venice*	(orator; judge; believes in justice)
Salarino	*The Merchant of Venice*	(confidant; caring; helps lovers)
Salanio	*The Merchant of Venice*	(confidant; caring; helps lovers)
Falstaff	*The Merry Wives of Windsor*	(delightfully debauched knight)
Ford	*The Merry Wives of Windsor*	(jealous husband in disguise)
Philostrate	*A Midsummer Night's Dream*	(master of revels; hates revels)
Theseus	*A Midsummer Night's Dream*	(authoritative, decisive, lover)
Antonio	*Much Ado about Nothing*	(loving uncle and father; wronged)
Benedick	*Much Ado about Nothing*	(witty brash soldier; bachelor)
Don John	*Much Ado about Nothing*	(sullen bastard; merciless villain)
Don Pedro	*Much Ado about Nothing*	(giving, concerned, loving leader)
Friar Francis	*Much Ado about Nothing*	(respected wise problem-solver)
Leonato	*Much Ado about Nothing*	(loving dad; irate when wronged)
Baptista	*The Taming of the Shrew*	(weary father turned dealmaker)
Gremio	*The Taming of the Shrew*	(aged competitive wooer; proud)
Hortensio	*The Taming of the Shrew*	(aged thwarted wooer; disguised)
Lord	*The Taming of the Shrew*	(virile, intelligent; plans trick)
Petruchio	*The Taming of the Shrew*	(swaggering gold-digger; lover)
Vincentio	*The Taming of the Shrew*	(aghast father; uncovers lies)
Alonso	*The Tempest*	(easily moved king; finds joy)
Antonio	*The Tempest*	(villainous brother; plots murder)
Gonzalo	*The Tempest*	(wise and trusted counselor)
Prospero	*The Tempest*	(sorcerer; avenger; father; wise)
Antonio	*The Two Gentlemen of Verona*	(authoritative decisive father)
Duke of Milan	*The Two Gentlemen of Verona*	(resenter; locks daughter in tower)
Sir Eglamour	*The Two Gentlemen of Verona*	(helpful; wistful; knows loss/love)

Thurio	*The Two Gentlemen of Verona*	(fop; fails to get girl; mockable)
Orsino	*Twelfth Night*	(mournful wooer; rash; romantic)
Sir Andrew Aguecheek	*Twelfth Night*	(foolish knight; spender; fop)
Sir Toby Belch	*Twelfth Night*	(grandiose drunk; loved; joker)
Antigonus	*The Winter's Tale*	(speaks unheard truths; loyal)
Camillo	*The Winter's Tale*	(loyal; refuses to murder; flees)
Cleomenes	*The Winter's Tale*	(noble; urges forgiveness; wise)
Dion	*The Winter's Tale*	(companion lord; urges reunion)
First Lord	*The Winter's Tale*	(begs on knees for reason; loyal)
Leontes	*The Winter's Tale*	(jealous; wrathful; mourns losses)
Polixenes	*The Winter's Tale*	(king; wrongly accused by friend)
Agrippa	*Antony and Cleopatra*	(officer; messenger; leads retreat)
Enobarbus	*Antony and Cleopatra*	(speaks passion; knows women)
Lepidus	*Antony and Cleopatra*	(urges reason and cool tempers)
Octavius	*Antony and Cleopatra*	(destined to be emperor; shrewd)
Ventidius	*Antony and Cleopatra*	(strong avenger; warring heart)
Cominius	*Coriolanus*	(mighty general; tells of bravery)
Coriolanus	*Coriolanus*	(valorous; prideful; indifferent)
First Lord	*Coriolanus*	(mournful; laments leader's death)
First Senator	*Coriolanus*	(loves Rome; witnesses attacks)
Junius Brutus	*Coriolanus*	(persuader of the people; tribune)
Menenius	*Coriolanus*	(powerful liaison; wise speaker)
Sicinius	*Coriolanus*	(power-thirsty tribune; betrayer)
Lartius	*Coriolanus*	(faithful general; loves his better)
Tullus Aufidius	*Coriolanus*	(mortal enemy turned truster)
Belarius	*Cymbeline*	(banished lord; steals twins)
Caius Lucius	*Cymbeline*	(noble respected general; Roman)
Cymbeline	*Cymbeline*	(wise and noble king; led astray)
First Gentleman	*Cymbeline*	(understands courtly history; tells)
Philario	*Cymbeline*	(generous kind host; loyal Italian)
Second Lord	*Cymbeline*	(astute noble; prays for princess)
Sicilius Leonatus	*Cymbeline*	(ghost; pleading warrior father)
Claudius	*Hamlet*	(plotting murderer; manipulator)
Ghost	*Hamlet*	(haunted; purgatory; vengeful)
Gentleman	*Hamlet*	(has seen disturbed woman)
Polonius	*Hamlet*	(social climber; babbler; father)
Priest	*Hamlet*	(holy; refuses sanctity to sinners)
Julius Caesar	*Julius Caesar*	(authoritative; arrogant; haunter)
Casca	*Julius Caesar*	(violently opposed to Caesar)

Flavius	*Julius Caesar*	(makes masses guilty; wise)
Murullus	*Julius Caesar*	(hot-tempered tribune; criticizes)
Duke of Albany	*King Lear*	(calls out betrayal; leads battles)
Duke of Cornwall	*King Lear*	(cruel; vile; wicked enabler)
Earl of Kent	*King Lear*	(true unto death; stands by king)
King of France	*King Lear*	(heart of gold; marries poor girl)
King Lear	*King Lear*	(father; madman; rash; volatile)
Duncan	*Macbeth*	(benevolent; trusting; unknowing)
Macbeth	*Macbeth*	(ambitious; manipulated; mad)
Macduff	*Macbeth*	(strong; true; loses all; just revenge)
Ross	*Macbeth*	(king's cousin; finally sees truth)
Siward	*Macbeth*	(stoic general strategist; loses son)
Duke of Venice	*Othello*	(authority, believes all will be well)
First Senator	*Othello*	(man of high standing; reasonable)
Montano	*Othello*	(governor; judge; just; fiery; hurt)
Roderigo	*Othello*	(lustful; manipulated; tattler; tool)
Capulet	*Romeo and Juliet*	(concerned with reputation; wrathful)
Montague	*Romeo and Juliet*	(concerned dad; worried; temper)
Paris	*Romeo and Juliet*	(rich suitor; quite the catch; fails)
Prince Escalus	*Romeo and Juliet*	(righteous anger; lays down law)
First Senator	*Timon of Athens*	(just; hard; not moved by speech)
First Stranger	*Timon of Athens*	(observant; warm; sees character)
Lucullus	*Timon of Athens*	(greedy non-friend; trickster; bad)
Old Athenian	*Timon of Athens*	(demands to pick daughter's man)
Second Senator	*Timon of Athens*	(tracks public opinion; astute)
Sempronius	*Timon of Athens*	(foppish; foolish; greedy turncoat)
Senator	*Timon of Athens*	(wants what he's owed; direct)
Timon	*Timon of Athens*	(generous to a fault; betrayed)
Ventidius	*Timon of Athens*	(makes show of returning money)
Marcus Andronicus	*Titus Andronicus*	(articulate tribune; wise; peaceful)
Saturninus	*Titus Andronicus*	(threatened ingrate; lustful; pomp)
Titus Andronicus	*Titus Andronicus*	(humble tragic hero; revenger)
Aeneas	*Troilus and Cressida*	(revered commander; bold; savvy)
Agamemnon	*Troilus and Cressida*	(Greek general: a violent windbag)
Diomedes	*Troilus and Cressida*	(commands; proud; woos; hates)
Nestor	*Troilus and Cressida*	(wise and aged general; counselor)
Pandarus	*Troilus and Cressida*	(uncle; bawdy; babbler; happy)
Priam	*Troilus and Cressida*	(king; heavyhearted; wise)
Ulysses	*Troilus and Cressida*	(powerful; speech giver; ambition)

Archbishop Scroop	*Henry IV, Part 1*	(priest turned rebel; predicts loss)
Archbishop Scroop	*Henry IV, Part 2*	("counterfeited zeal"; rebel leader)
Earl of Westmorland	*Henry IV, Part 1*	(king's companion; loyal)
Earl of Westmorland	*Henry IV, Part 2*	(king's man; loyal; captures rebels)
Earl of Worcester	*Henry IV, Part 1*	(disloyal; manipulates; secrets)
Sir John Falstaff	*Henry IV, Part 1*	(riotous; drinker; eater; lover; fat)
Sir John Falstaff	*Henry IV, Part 2*	(aging drunken wit; ill; banished)
King Henry IV	*Henry IV, Part 1*	(exhausted king; dissolute son)
King Henry IV	*Henry IV, Part 2*	(failing health; embattled; dies)
Mortimer	*Henry IV, Part 1*	(captured; loves wife; accused)
Vernon	*Henry IV, Part 1*	(noble; rebel; reason; secrets kept)
Earl of Northumberland	*Henry IV, Part 2*	(feigns illness; loses son; rebel)
Earl of Warwick	*Henry IV, Part 2*	(king's ally; reasonable; sees truth)
Lord Bardolph	*Henry IV, Part 2*	(brings false news; describes war)
Lord Chief Justice	*Henry IV, Part 2*	(father figure; advisor; trusted)
Lord Hastings	*Henry IV, Part 2*	(conspirator; "time's subject")
Archbishop of Canterbury	*Henry V*	(reasonable; urges invasion)
Bishop of Ely	*Henry V*	(passionate; eloquent; urges war)
Constable of France	*Henry V*	(unabashedly French; arrogant)
Duke of Bourbon	*Henry V*	(flees enemy; rouses courage)
Duke of Burgundy	*Henry V*	(arranges meeting of kings; peace)
Duke of Exeter	*Henry V*	(eloquent; brings fiery war words)
Earl of Salisbury	*Henry V*	(valiant force leader; charges on!)
Earl of Westmorland	*Henry V*	(strategist; understands politics)
Governor of Harfleur	*Henry V*	(admits graceful sorrowful defeat)
Gower	*Henry V*	(no-nonsense leader; defends)
Grandpré	*Henry V*	(laments carnage on French field)
King of France	*Henry V*	(does not underestimate enemy)
Bastard of Orléans	*Henry VI, Part 1*	(talent scout; believes in miracles)
Duke of Bedford	*Henry VI, Part 1*	(leads army while dying in chair)
Duke of Burgundy	*Henry VI, Part 1*	(defects for France; won over)
Duke of Exeter	*Henry VI, Part 1*	(urges blood; bitter commentary)
Gloucester	*Henry VI, Part 1*	(protector of the realm; fight; zeal)
Mortimer	*Henry VI, Part 1*	(claim to throne; imprisoned; age)
General	*Henry VI, Part 1*	(rouses men for terrible war)
Lord Talbot	*Henry VI, Part 1*	(general; true; guarded by archers)
Mayor of London	*Henry VI, Part 1*	(desperate; warfare in his city)
Sir William Lucy	*Henry VI, Part 1*	(dismayed; private quarrels harm)
Winchester	*Henry VI, Part 1*	(ambition; power; soon cardinal)

Alexander Iden	*Henry VI, Part 2*	(prefers home to city; forced kill)
Duke of Buckingham	*Henry VI, Part 2*	(ambition; loyalty; witch hunter)
Gloucester	*Henry VI, Part 2*	(ambition; defender; murder abed)
Earl of Salisbury	*Henry VI, Part 2*	(cares for kingdom and people)
Father John Hume	*Henry VI, Part 2*	(blinded by gold love; manipulate)
Lord Clifford	*Henry VI, Part 2*	(heals divisions with speech; wise)
Lord Say	*Henry VI, Part 2*	(educated; bilingual; mob blames)
Richard Plantagenet	*Henry VI, Part 1*	(father disgraced; honor regained)
Richard Plantagenet	*Henry VI, Part 2*	(believes he'd make better king)
Humphrey Stafford	*Henry VI, Part 2*	(raises army; attacks fleeing poor)
Winchester	*Henry VI, Part 2*	(liar; jealous hatred; cardinal; evil)
Somerset	*Henry VI, Part 1*	(classist; haughty; despises Yorks)
Earl of Northumberland	*Henry VI, Part 3*	(compares enemies to dogs)
Earl of Warwick	*Henry VI, Part 3*	(fierce; arrogant; a kingmaker)
Henry VI	*Henry VI, Part 3*	(kind man in midst of war; holy)
Lord Clifford	*Henry VI, Part 3*	(cruel sadist; seeks revenge; dies)
Richard Plantagenet	*Henry VI, Part 3*	(loses crown; bitter; heartbroken)
Archbishop Cranmer	*Henry VIII*	(integrity; close to king; heart)
Cardinal Wolsey	*Henry VIII*	(butcher's son has power; wily)
Duke of Buckingham	*Henry VIII*	(eloquent snob; accused of treason)
Duke of Norfolk	*Henry VIII*	(has rod of authority; calm; wise)
Duke of Suffolk	*Henry VIII*	(High Steward; very close to king)
Griffith	*Henry VIII*	(gateway to queen; cares deeply)
Henry VIII	*Henry VIII*	(gives cardinal power; entraps)
Lord Chamberlain	*Henry VIII*	(loyal; chauvinist; hates French)
Lord Chancellor	*Henry VIII*	(seals laws; authority; gets it done)
Sir Thomas Lovell	*Henry VIII*	(foppish complaining knight)
Cardinal Pandulph	*King John*	(manipulates; political; cold heart)
King John	*King John*	(weakling; too ambitious; murdered)
Philip King of France	*King John*	(switches sides like flipping coin)
Lymoges	*King John*	(king killing braggart; wears lion skin)
Melun	*King John*	(French; helps English as dying)
Antiochus	*Pericles*	(incestuous; foul; wicked; devious)
Cerimon	*Pericles*	(respected healer; kind; wise)
Cleon	*Pericles*	(weak governor; allows murder; starving)
Helicanus	*Pericles*	(trusted counselor; humble; loyal)
Lysimachus	*Pericles*	(converted by maiden purity)
Pericles	*Pericles*	(good heart; bad luck; all restored)
Simonides	*Pericles*	(kindly father; tests love; blesses)

Abbot	*Richard II*	(grieved by unholy; plans murder)
Bishop of Carlisle	*Richard II*	(speaks his mind; honest; prophet)
Duke of Surrey	*Richard II*	(knows a liar when he hears one)
Edmund of Langley	*Richard II*	(old; well-meaning; ineffective)
John of Gaunt	*Richard II*	(loved; respected; wealthy; wise)
Richard II	*Richard II*	(steals; taxes; flowery speeches)
Thomas Mowbray	*Richard II*	(patriot; supports nobility; exile)
Cardinal Bourchier	*Richard III*	(humble; entreats; avoids sin)
Duke of Buckingham	*Richard III*	(maneuverer; outmaneuvered)
King Edward IV	*Richard III*	(ailing; fears God's judgment)
Earl Rivers	*Richard III*	(his advice ignored; dies well)
Lord Hastings	*Richard III*	(ignores portents; too trusting)
Richmond	*Richard III*	(Henry VII; slays evil; unites; wins)
Lord Stanley	*Richard III*	(caught in intrigue; crowns king)

YOUNGER TO MIDDLE-AGED MEN (LOW STATUS)

Clown	*All's Well That Ends Well*	(bawdy joker, serves women well)
Steward	*All's Well That Ends Well*	(faithful servant; eavesdropper)
Touchstone	*As You Like It*	(bawdy companion clown)
Silvius	*As You Like It*	(desperate love-struck shepherd)
Angelo	*The Comedy of Errors*	(disgruntled polite goldsmith)
Antipholus of Ephesus	*The Comedy of Errors*	(irate husband; violent meltdown)
Antipholus of Syracuse	*The Comedy of Errors*	(bewildered seeker of lost brother)
Dromio of Ephesus	*The Comedy of Errors*	(clown slave; beaten but tough)
Dromio of Syracuse	*The Comedy of Errors*	(clown slave; ugly woman chases)
Boyet	*Love's Labour's Lost*	(amused lord serves princess)
Costard	*Love's Labour's Lost*	(love-rival clown; plays tricks)
Moth	*Love's Labour's Lost*	(observant witty servant)
Elbow	*Measure for Measure*	(a simple constable; malapropic)
Pompey	*Measure for Measure*	(clownish rambler; serves bawd)
Clerk	*The Merchant of Venice*	(official of the court; good reader)
Launcelot Gobbo	*The Merchant of Venice*	(puny clown; once-jilted servant)
Flute	*A Midsummer Night's Dream*	(adolescent unwillingly plays girl)
Borachio	*Much Ado about Nothing*	(deceitful conspirator; repents)
Biondello	*The Taming of the Shrew*	(energetic confused servant)
Grumio	*The Taming of the Shrew*	(beaten servant: confused, jolly)
Messenger	*The Taming of the Shrew*	(convincing; dramatic; flourishes)
Tranio	*The Taming of the Shrew*	(streetwise servant trickster pal)
Stephano	*The Tempest*	(drunken servant; becomes boss)

Trinculo	*The Tempest*	(drunken jester; mocks monsters)
First Outlaw	*The Two Gentlemen of Verona*	(threatening, inviting, direct)
Speed	*The Two Gentlemen of Verona*	(playful; loyal; mocks lovers)
Third Outlaw	*The Two Gentlemen of Verona*	(tough; deferential; seeks a king)
Valentine	*Twelfth Night*	(efficient servant; social climber)
Clown	*The Winter's Tale*	(buffoon; loving put-upon brother)
Lord	*The Winter's Tale*	(loyal messenger; delivers drama)
Second Lord	*The Winter's Tale*	(excited witness of greatness)
Servant	*The Winter's Tale*	(gossipy reporter of details)
Alexas	*Antony and Cleopatra*	(servant: brings flattering missive)
Clown	*Antony and Cleopatra*	(bawdy jokester; poison bringer)
Dercetas	*Antony and Cleopatra*	(just swordsman; sees murder)
Diomedes	*Antony and Cleopatra*	(Alas! Brings good news too late)
Eros	*Antony and Cleopatra*	(sad; refuses to murder master)
Mardian	*Antony and Cleopatra*	(eunuch; witnesses queen's death)
Menas	*Antony and Cleopatra*	(seeks permission to murder)
Messenger	*Antony and Cleopatra*	(brings disturbing news; watches)
Philo	*Antony and Cleopatra*	(soldier; hates Antony's weakness)
Proculeius	*Antony and Cleopatra*	(soldier; prevents a suicide; kind)
Scarus	*Antony and Cleopatra*	(oft wounded in battle; sees all)
Silius	*Antony and Cleopatra*	(loyal; urges others to action)
First Citizen	*Coriolanus*	(brave; defies authority; speaker)
First Officer	*Coriolanus*	(shrewd observer of ill-favor)
First Servingman	*Coriolanus*	(claims he prefers war to peace)
Lieutenant	*Coriolanus*	(worried; urges leader onward)
Messenger	*Coriolanus*	(has seen amazing things; reports)
Roman	*Coriolanus*	(brings strange wondrous tidings)
Second Messenger	*Coriolanus*	(Huzzah! News of joyful victory!)
Third Servingman	*Coriolanus*	(has the dirt on the politicians)
First Gaoler	*Cymbeline*	(comedic; sees benefits of hanging)
Pisanio	*Cymbeline*	(faithful servant; defends honor)
Posthumus	*Cymbeline*	(orphan; lover; moved to anger)
Horatio	*Hamlet*	(scholar; faithful friend; intellect)
Marcellus	*Hamlet*	(superstitious; non-scholar)
Messenger	*Hamlet*	(Sees the impending army! Run!)
Osric	*Hamlet*	(courtier; gushes about gentles)
Rosencrantz	*Hamlet*	(social climber serves king; lies)
(Decius) Brutus	*Julius Caesar*	(false interpreter of dreams)
Ligarius	*Julius Caesar*	(poetical; passionate conspirator)

Messala	*Julius Caesar*	(mourning server; brings ill news)
Pindarus	*Julius Caesar*	(watches master's murder at field)
Servant	*Julius Caesar*	(begs for forgiveness for master)
Tintinius	*Julius Caesar*	(officer; suicides when leader dies)
Edmund	*King Lear*	(bastard; bitter betrayer; intellect)
Oswald	*King Lear*	(fiery; quick to draw; mailman)
Lennox	*Macbeth*	(observes strange downfalls)
Messenger	*Macbeth*	(fleet of foot; tries to warn; scared)
Sergeant	*Macbeth*	(tells riveting tale; bleeding)
Cassio	*Othello*	(charming courtly lieutenant; flirt)
Herald	*Othello*	(ebullient; bearer of glad tidings)
Iago	*Othello*	(competitive; deceitful; vengeful)
Second Gentleman	*Othello*	(delivers dramatic war news)
Balthasar	*Romeo and Juliet*	(servant sees woeful things; upset)
Peter	*Romeo and Juliet*	(playful abused servant; coward)
Servant	*Romeo and Juliet*	(illiterate; tenacious; eager; rush)
Flaminius	*Timon of Athens*	(fiery servant; scathing in rebukes)
Lucilius	*Timon of Athens*	(servant; sorrows for master)
Painter	*Timon of Athens*	(gold-digging; false; manipulative)
Poet	*Timon of Athens*	(gold-digging; false; pretty lies)
Second Servant	*Timon of Athens*	(witnesses betrayals; heart-heavy)
Servant	*Timon of Athens*	(astounded at world's cruel greed)
Servilius	*Timon of Athens*	(pleads for unwell master; true)
Third Servant	*Timon of Athens*	(makes loyal stand for fallen boss)
Messenger	*Titus Andronicus*	(aghast at cruelty; painful news)
Second Goth	*Titus Andronicus*	(daydreamer; overhears evidence)
Alexander	*Troilus and Cressida*	(chatty servant; likes to dish)
Patroclus	*Troilus and Cressida*	(pretty boy; coward; influencer)
Edward (Ned) Poins	*Henry IV, Part 1*	(criminal; trickster; friend)
Edward (Ned) Poins	*Henry IV, Part 2*	(trickster; pal; prince's confidant)
Gadshill	*Henry IV, Part 1*	(spy; thief; friend; mocks hanging)
Second Carrier	*Henry IV, Part 1*	(flea-bitten; broke; hates house)
Davy	*Henry IV, Part 2*	(faithful servant; pleads for friend)
Travers	*Henry IV, Part 2*	(servant brings joyful tidings)
Boy	*Henry V*	(knows manhood; dislikes knaves)
First Ambassador	*Henry V*	(messenger delivers cruel joke)
Williams	*Henry V*	(plain-talking soldier; truth; bold)
Bassett	*Henry VI, Part 1*	(wants to duel over his red rose)
Jack Cade	*Henry VI, Part 2*	(commoner posing king; FIGHTS)

Messenger	*Henry VI, Part 2*	(flees for his life; brings news)
Messenger	*Henry VI, Part 3*	(tells of brutality; bloody hankies)
Son	*Henry VI, Part 3*	(has killed his own father; grieves)
Surveyor	*Henry VIII*	(loses job; accuses boss of treason)
English Herald	*King John*	(jubilant; articulate; The winners!)
First Citizen	*King John*	(speaks cannon fire even to kings)
French Herald	*King John*	(announces victory to the public)
Boult	*Pericles*	(would-be rapist; gross; ad man)
Leonine	*Pericles*	(would-be murderer; hidden heart)
Thaliard	*Pericles*	(murderer on the hunt; cunning)
Bagot	*Richard II*	(commoner close to king; brave)
Bushy	*Richard II*	(commoner close to king; suave)
Groom	*Richard II*	(loves horses and deposed king)
Sir Pierce of Exton	*Richard II*	(fool knight; murders unbidden)
Fourth Messenger	*Richard II*	(brings news of bad king's folly)
Second Murderer	*Richard III*	(hardened; bout of conscience)
Sir Richard Ratcliff	*Richard III*	(faithful executioner; serves evil)

MIDDLE-AGED TO OLDER MEN (LOW STATUS)

Clown	*All's Well That Ends Well*	(bawdy joker; serves women well)
Steward	*All's Well That Ends Well*	(faithful servant eavesdropper)
Touchstone	*As You Like It*	(bawdy companion clown)
Charles	*As You Like It*	(caring savvy strongman)
Adam	*As You Like It*	(faithful elderly servant gives all)
Corin	*As You Like It*	(rejected love-counsel shepherd)
Egeon/Aegeon	*The Comedy of Errors*	(grieving jailed merchant)
Angelo	*The Comedy of Errors*	(disgruntled polite goldsmith)
Balthazar	*The Comedy of Errors*	(calm merchant prevents violence)
Costard	*Love's Labour's Lost*	(love-rival clown; plays tricks)
Friar Peter	*Measure for Measure*	(honest observer defends truth)
Provost	*Measure for Measure*	(hand of justice; demands truth)
Shylock	*The Merchant of Venice*	(abused Jew; seeks revenge)
Doctor Caius	*The Merry Wives of Windsor*	(absurdly French suitor; choleric)
Host	*The Merry Wives of Windsor*	(wild mocker; victim of revenge)
Nym	*The Merry Wives of Windsor*	(bedraggled bringer of truth)
Sir Hugh Evans	*The Merry Wives of Windsor*	(mocked Welsh pastor; revenge)
Bottom	*A Midsummer Night's Dream*	(histrionic grand yokel; in love)
Egeus	*A Midsummer Night's Dream*	(irate father condemns daughter)
Quince	*A Midsummer Night's Dream*	(frazzled would-be director)

Snout	*A Midsummer Night's Dream*	(tinker; the type to play a wall)
Snug	*A Midsummer Night's Dream*	(cowardly; forced to play the lion)
Dogberry	*Much Ado about Nothing*	(earnest foolish bumbler of law)
Christopher Sly	*The Taming of the Shrew*	(drunk insulter; thinks he's a lord)
Pedant	*The Taming of the Shrew*	(nervous; credulous; disguised)
Boatswain	*The Tempest*	(hardy; skillful; sees miracles)
Francisco	*The Tempest*	(amazed sailor; brings hope)
Launce	*The Two Gentlemen of Verona*	(devoted to mutt; tragicomic)
Panthino	*The Two Gentlemen of Verona*	(wise servant; advises duke)
Antonio	*Twelfth Night*	(loyal; hot-tempered; betrayed)
Captain	*Twelfth Night*	(kind; hopeful; risk-taker)
Fabian	*Twelfth Night*	(jovial trickster; convincing)
Feste	*Twelfth Night*	(a witty fool; singer of sad songs)
Malvolio	*Twelfth Night*	(pretentious lovelorn steward)
Autolycus	*The Winter's Tale*	(rogue; thief; clown; assists lovers)
Officer	*The Winter's Tale*	(threatening authority figure)
Old Shepherd	*The Winter's Tale*	(honorable; wizened; nurtures)
Third Gentleman	*The Winter's Tale*	(witness of wondrous things)
Canidius	*Antony and Cleopatra*	(witnesses destruction and defeat)
Dolabella	*Antony and Cleopatra*	(regretful; guards captured queen)
Soldier	*Antony and Cleopatra*	(urges land war rather than sea)
Soothsayer	*Antony and Cleopatra*	(enigmatic medium; warns)
Second Officer	*Coriolanus*	(offers astute political comments)
Third Citizen	*Coriolanus*	(bold rouser of the people; fiery)
Cornelius	*Cymbeline*	(astute doctor; switches potions)
Soothsayer	*Cymbeline*	(enigmatic medium; warns)
Gravedigger/Clown	*Hamlet*	(macabre; jovial skull-toucher)
First Player	*Hamlet*	(skillful actor; can cry on demand)
Player King	*Hamlet*	(senses an impending betrayal)
Voltemand	*Hamlet*	(courtier brings false hope to king)
Artemidorus	*Julius Caesar*	(loyal; desperate to save Caesar)
Lucillius	*Julius Caesar*	(soldier sees carnage; defends)
Second Commoner	*Julius Caesar*	(humble celebrating shoemaker)
Fool	*King Lear*	(truth speaker/mocker; most sane)
Gentleman	*King Lear*	(fearful witness of courtly terrors)
Angus	*Macbeth*	(gleefully reports downfalls; just)
Banquo	*Macbeth*	(general; promoted; moral; true)
Doctor	*Macbeth*	(observer; signs in nature; disturbed)
Lord	*Macbeth*	(remembers better times; reports)

Porter	*Macbeth*	(drunk)
Othello	*Othello*	(soldier; jealous; loves; rash)
Watchman	*Romeo and Juliet*	(finds carnage; rapid investigator)
Friar Laurence	*Romeo and Juliet*	(naturalist; potions; wise; unwise)
Friar John	*Romeo and Juliet*	(mendicant; happy; fails delivery)
Alcibiades	*Timon of Athens*	(soldier of mercy; pleads; avenges)
Apemantus	*Timon of Athens*	(churlish philosopher; bitter)
Flavius	*Timon of Athens*	(dedicated accountant; true heart)
Fool	*Timon of Athens*	(compares lenders to prostitutes)
Soldier	*Timon of Athens*	(finds tomb; mourns lost lord)
Aaron	*Titus Andronicus*	(well-spoken sexual predator; vile)
First Goth	*Titus Andronicus*	(zealous; has waited for revenge)
Calchas	*Troilus and Cressida*	(holy man turned beggar; pleads)
Thersites	*Troilus and Cressida*	(rude; bitter; bellicose; rails)
Blunt	*Henry IV, Part 1*	(loyal; killed disguised as king)
Chamberlain	*Henry IV, Part 1*	(harried; has the dirt on visitors)
Owen Glendower	*Henry IV, Part 1*	(Welsh rebel; claims mystic ways)
Bardolph	*Henry IV, Part 2*	(red-nosed drinker; degenerate)
Francis Feeble	*Henry IV, Part 2*	(women's tailor forced to soldier)
Morton	*Henry IV, Part 2*	(brings heartbreaking war news)
Pistol	*Henry IV, Part 2*	(brawl; swagger; boast; loud)
Justice Shallow	*Henry IV, Part 2*	(rambler; relives glory days)
Captain Fluellen	*Henry V*	(passionately Welsh; verbose)
Captain Macmorris	*Henry V*	(passion; Irish; Fight! Not talk!)
Montjoy	*Henry V*	(herald; bold French threats)
Pistol	*Henry V*	(histrionic speaker; faces sorrow)
Master-Gunner	*Henry VI, Part 1*	(overworked; keeps watch; leaves)
Messenger	*Henry VI, Part 1*	(sad story at funeral; rouses)
Officer	*Henry VI, Part 1*	(demands disarmament; order)
Shepherd	*Henry VI, Part 1*	(curses disobedient daughter)
Bolingbroke	*Henry VI, Part 2*	(conjurer; wizard; of the night)
Captain	*Henry VI, Part 2*	(hard sea captain; executes at sea)
Peter	*Henry VI, Part 2*	(common; duels with drunk; wins)
Thomas Horner	*Henry VI, Part 2*	(falsely accused by apprentice)
Vaux	*Henry VI, Part 2*	(messenger mourns ill cardinal)
Walter Whitmore	*Henry VI, Part 2*	(one-eyed pirate; fierce; feared)
Father	*Henry VI, Part 3*	(unwittingly murders son; grieves)
Porter's Man	*Henry VIII*	(ineffective crowd control; tries)
Porter	*Henry VIII*	(fights losing battle against mob)

Hubert de Burgh	*King John*	(wise citizen; tricky; kind heart)
First Fisherman	*Pericles*	(wry; sense of humor; judges rich)
Captain	*Richard II*	(abandons post; thinks king dead)
Gardener	*Richard II*	(apt metaphors; wise; empathetic)
Servant	*Richard II*	(poor memory; brings sad news)
Messenger	*Richard III*	(informer; delivers dreams)
Scrivener	*Richard III*	(writes lies beautifully; sees truth)
Sir James Tyrell	*Richard III*	(lowly knight; murderer; regret)
Sir Robert Brackenbury	*Richard III*	(runs tower; faithful to any king)
Sir William Catesby	*Richard III*	(faithful; begs for rescue; rejected)

YOUNGER TO MIDDLE-AGED WOMEN (HIGH STATUS)

Helena	*All's Well That Ends Well*	(love-struck; determined heart)
Rosalind	*As You Like It*	(independent; clever; x-dresser)
Celia	*As You Like It*	(devoted friend; rejects cruel dad)
Princess of France	*Love's Labour's Lost*	(intelligent political princess; flirt)
Maria	*Love's Labour's Lost*	(smart flirty lady; gets her guy)
Katherine	*Love's Labour's Lost*	(smart flirty lady; gets her guy)
Rosaline	*Love's Labour's Lost*	(smart flirty lady; gets her guy)
Isabella	*Measure for Measure*	(pure; pleads for brother's life)
Nerissa	*The Merchant of Venice*	(jovial; wise; lady-in-waiting)
Portia	*The Merchant of Venice*	(wise; brave; in love; x-dresses)
Helena	*A Midsummer Night's Dream*	(desperate jilted gal; betrays, begs)
Hermia	*A Midsummer Night's Dream*	(eloping daughter; friend betrays)
Beatrice	*Much Ado about Nothing*	(witty, bold, rejects most men)
Hero	*Much Ado about Nothing*	(sweet, vulnerable, wronged)
Bianca	*The Taming of the Shrew*	(sweet-seeming beautiful flirt)
Katherine	*The Taming of the Shrew*	(shrewish-seeming; smart, strong)
Miranda	*The Tempest*	(unworldly; empathetic; romantic)
Julia	*The Two Gentlemen of Verona*	(adores her cheating man; x-dress)
Silvia	*The Two Gentlemen of Verona*	(virtuous; steadfast; rejects falsity)
Olivia	*Twelfth Night*	(mournful; disdainful; wild in love)
Viola	*Twelfth Night*	(true; wise; loving; bold; x-dresses)
Perdita	*The Winter's Tale*	(disguised princess shepherdess)
Imogen	*Cymbeline*	(wise; resourceful; determined)
Ophelia	*Hamlet*	(vulnerable; in love; mad; loses all)
Portia	*Julius Caesar*	(courageous strong-willed wife)
Cordelia	*King Lear*	(truthful daughter; kind princess)
Goneril	*King Lear*	(eldest; betrayer; poisoner; cold)

Regan	*King Lear*	(betrayer; stabs a man; murdered)
Desdemona	*Othello*	(passion; pure; loves heroic tales)
Juliet	*Romeo and Juliet*	(pure; passionate; bold; despair)
Lavinia	*Titus Andronicus*	(chaste general's daughter; pretty)
Cassandra	*Troilus and Cressida*	(prophetess; princess; cursed)
Cressida	*Troilus and Cressida*	(beautiful; smart; smitten; false)
Lady Percy	*Henry IV, Part 1*	(direct wife; wants sex; neglected)
Lady Percy	*Henry IV, Part 2*	(direct daughter; begs not to fight)
Katharine	*Henry V*	(chaste; blushes easily; French)
Margaret	*Henry VI, Part 2*	(gains power over weak husband)
Anne Bullen	*Henry VIII*	(wins masked king; sweet; elopes)
Blanch	*King John*	(highly obedient; naive; pleads)
Marina	*Pericles*	(pure; talented; hidden princess)
Thaisa	*Pericles*	(princess; loves; mourns; regains)
Queen	*Richard II*	(French; tries to join hubby in jail)
Lady Anne	*Richard III*	(seduced by murderer; betrayed)

MIDDLE-AGED TO OLDER WOMEN (HIGH STATUS)

Countess	*All's Well That Ends Well*	(wise defender of wronged girl)
Mistress Ford	*The Merry Wives of Windsor*	(faithful wife; gleefully humiliates)
Mistress Page	*The Merry Wives of Windsor*	(arguing wife; gleefully humiliates)
Hippolyta	*A Midsummer Night's Dream*	(hot Amazon queen; engaged)
Emilia	*The Winter's Tale*	(concerned nursemaid; good)
Hermione	*The Winter's Tale*	(long-suffering virtuous queen)
Paulina	*The Winter's Tale*	(bold well-spoken defender; wise)
Cleopatra	*Antony and Cleopatra*	(seducer: mercurial suicide queen)
Octavia	*Antony and Cleopatra*	(torn between hubby and brother)
Valeria	*Coriolanus*	(dotes on children; go-getter)
Volumnia	*Coriolanus*	(mom overbears; ambitious; war)
Queen	*Cymbeline*	(wicked stepmother; poisoner)
Gertrude	*Hamlet*	(wife of murderer; inscrutably regal)
Calpurnia	*Julius Caesar*	(prophetic wife; begs for safety)
Lady Macbeth	*Macbeth*	(ambitious; driven; cold; insane)
Lady Macduff	*Macbeth*	(kindly mother; playful; sweet)
Lady Capulet	*Romeo and Juliet*	(eager matchmaker; wed young)
Tamora	*Titus Andronicus*	(dark queen; revenges child; allure)
Queen Isabel	*Henry V*	(willing matchmaker; hopeful)
Countess of Auvergne	*Henry VI, Part 1*	(lays man trap; obsessive; threats)
Eleanor of Gloucester	*Henry VI, Part 2*	(belittles; mocks; proud; tricked)

Queen Margaret	*Henry VI, Part 3*	(love for son drives; desperate)
Lady Grey/Queen Elizabeth	*Henry VI, Part 3*	(wildly promoted; disgusts nobles)
Queen Katherine	*Henry VIII*	(betrayed by hubby/church; divorce)
Constance	*King John*	(temper; wants her son as king)
Queen Elinor	*King John*	(clever; spy; flirt; near death; bold)
Dionyza	*Pericles*	(evil queen; plots; mirror mirror)
Duchess of Gloucester	*Richard II*	(grieving widow seeks help: none)
Duchess of York	*Richard II*	(she must save accused only son)
Duchess of York	*Richard III*	(mom of monster; curses; rage)
Queen Elizabeth	*Richard III*	(fights to save children; suffers)
Queen Margaret	*Richard III*	(curses; wrath; sustaining hate)

YOUNGER TO MIDDLE-AGED WOMEN (LOW STATUS)

Diana Capilet	*All's Well That Ends Well*	(chaste; shuns men; tricks cad)
Phoebe	*As You Like It*	(desperate love-struck sheep gal)
Adriana	*The Comedy of Errors*	(irate wronged wife; loses it)
Courtesan	*The Comedy of Errors*	(sultry trickster out for cash)
Luciana	*The Comedy of Errors*	(chaste sister chased by man)
Francisca	*Measure for Measure*	(pure nun; won't speak to men)
Mariana	*Measure for Measure*	(jilted fiancée pulls the bed trick)
Jessica	*The Merchant of Venice*	(unhappy daughter; steals; elopes)
Charmian	*Antony and Cleopatra*	(girlish servant; mourns queen)
Joan la Pucelle	*Henry VI, Part 1*	(demons; visions; shepherd; war)

MIDDLE-AGED TO OLDER WOMEN (LOW STATUS)

Widow	*All's Well That Ends Well*	(cunning; pure; tricks cad)
Mariana	*All's Well That Ends Well*	(good neighbor; warns about cads)
Emilia/Abbess	*The Comedy of Errors*	(suffering mom turned bossy nun)
Mistress Overdone	*Measure for Measure*	(bawdy madam; cares for kids)
Hostess Quickly	*The Merry Wives of Windsor*	(perceives innuendo often; rushes)
Margaret	*Much Ado about Nothing*	(servant; playful, wanton at night)
Maria	*Twelfth Night*	(playful scolding witty wench)
Player Queen	*Hamlet*	(wrongly protests her faithfulness)
Bianca	*Othello*	(hooker; seamstress; pawn; irate)
Emilia	*Othello*	(loyal handmaid; betraying hubby)
Nurse	*Romeo and Juliet*	(happy babbler; motherly; bawdy)
Hostess Quickly	*Henry IV, Part 1*	(runs tavern; shrewish; bold)
Hostess Quickly	*Henry IV, Part 2*	(dim-witted; kindhearted; owed)
Doll Tearsheet	*Henry IV, Part 2*	(prostitute; knife fights, saucy)

Hostess Quickly	*Henry V*	(sees death of beloved one; loss)
Old Woman	*Henry VIII*	(bawdy money-grubbing rudesby)
Bawd	*Pericles*	(not impressed with virginity)

AGELESS CREATURES OF ANOTHER WORLD (HIGH STATUS)

Hymen	*As You Like It*	(joyful god of marriage)
Oberon	*A Midsummer Night's Dream*	(powerful jealous angry romantic)
Titania	*A Midsummer Night's Dream*	(powerful donkey-smitten queen)
Ceres	*The Tempest*	(regal grain goddess; blesses)
Iris	*The Tempest*	(rainbow goddess; blesses)
Time	*The Winter's Tale*	(chorus; indulgent; storyteller)
Jupiter	*Cymbeline*	(thunderer; provides deliverance)
Hecate	*Macbeth*	(haughty; powerful; schemer)
Rumour	*Henry IV, Part 2*	(chorus; haughty; commanding)
Diana	*Pericles*	(pure; goddess of chastity; helps)
Gower	*Pericles*	(ghost of ancient storyteller; poet)
Henry VI	*Richard III*	(ghost; comes to curse and uplift)
Princes	*Richard III*	(ghosts; come to haunt and help)

AGELESS CREATURES OF ANOTHER WORLD (LOW STATUS)

First Fairy	*A Midsummer Night's Dream*	(busy sprite; knows her goblins)
Puck	*A Midsummer Night's Dream*	(playful impish hobgoblin)
Ariel	*The Tempest*	(swift elemental in sad bondage)
Caliban	*The Tempest*	(boorish supplanted witch-spawn)
First Witch	*Macbeth*	(serves devil; mystery; vengeful)
Second Witch	*Macbeth*	(serves devil; mystery; cook)
Third Witch	*Macbeth*	(serves devil; mystery; cook)
Chorus	*Romeo and Juliet*	(knows all; tells all; begs favor)
Chorus	*Troilus and Cressida*	(brings us into the strife of war)
Dancer	*Henry IV, Part 2*	(dances; apologizes; gives teaser)
Chorus	*Henry V*	(eloquent; poet; pleads: imagine!)
Chorus	*Henry VIII*	(humble; faults; warns sadness)

SONNETS: THE DARK HORSE AUDITION PIECES

Actors often ask, "What about the sonnets? Can't I just use one of those for my audition?" Well, the answer is . . . maybe.

Sonnets are appealing because they are already whole; they don't ever require cutting, and they always come in at a perfectly succinct fourteen lines. They have lovely rhyming couplets at their closes, which gives each piece a strong ending and makes it sound complete. These poems are beautifully written and contain high drama and melancholy. There are also 154 of them to choose from, only three of which most people seem to know (Steer clear of: "Shall I compare thee to a summer's day?", "Let me not to the marriage of true minds admit impediments," and "When in disgrace with fortune and men's eyes"). You don't have to read a whole play (or even a whole scene) to understand the sonnets. What's not to love?

The challenge with sonnets is that they don't always give an actor a strong situation or context. We can't always tell where you are, who you are talking to, or what your driving goal might be. I once sat in on auditions with the casting director of the California Shakespeare Theater, and she was always dissatisfied when an actor brought in a sonnet, because it just didn't show her enough of what she needed to know: can this person convince me they have a certain status? Can this person pursue a driving goal on stage?

To combat this, it helps to be aware that the sonnets *do* seem to tell a kind of story (albeit a much-debated one). The story even has characters: the poet, the young man, and the dark lady. These three interact in various ways:

- The poet praises the young man and urges him to marry and have children.
- The young man betrays the poet.
- The dark lady appears as a rival.
- The poet forgives and endures.

Along the way there are revelations, tortured confessions, and beautiful sentiments. However, these don't necessarily play out on stage.

That being said, I have seen actors interpret the Shakespeare sonnets with heartbreaking truthfulness. I have seen them move audiences to tears.

So, should you audition with a sonnet?

Answer: Only if it's really *good*.

6. Next Steps

Now you understand the categories of plays. You've identified your type. You have an idea of which characters in which plays might be a match for your specific age and type.

What do you do next?

Now you need to do some of the work that you'd have to do for any audition. So let's figure out how you want to be seen for this particular audition.

To do this, let's look at two different instances where you'll need a classical piece:

- Auditions where you will be considered for casting in a specific Shakespeare play
- Group auditions for multiple theatres, or auditions for training programs (i.e. cases where you are not auditioning for a specific play, but need to show your classical work)

Let's look first at the first instance: auditions for a specific play.

Let's pretend that SummerStockExtravaganza Theatre Company is casting their summer season. They're doing a bunch of musicals (and let's say that's your main area of strength). As part of their summer season they're doing what many summer theatres often do–including a crowd-pleasing outdoor summer Shakespeare play. They will be casting *Much Ado about Nothing.*

You've looked at the character descriptions for the play (something that you should always do, of course, for any audition that you go to) and you think you're the best fit for the role of the character Hero. Hero is a sweet young thing. She's described as kind and gentle, and she's clearly high-status. A quick flip through the text and you can see that she speaks in verse.

Much Ado about Nothing is one of Shakespeare's comedies, so knowing who Hero is and what category of play she appears in, your best bet is to use the guide in the previous chapter to find another Shakespeare comedy with another sweet young thing. Does this other sweet young thing in another Shakespeare comedy have a nice chunk of verse to speak? Shakespeare's comedies are filled with many characters of similar type. If you spend any time with Hero in *Much Ado*, you will quickly learn that she is not a laugh-a-minute; she's a little more bland and vanilla than Shakespeare's other sweet young things. Still, you will see similarities between Hero and many of Shakespeare's other young heroines. A scan through similar status and age types in Shakespeare's comedies will reveal to you that *All's Well That Ends Well* includes the lovely character Helena (who has a beautiful monologue in Act 1, scene 3.) Although Helena is a little snazzier than Hero (sorry, Hero) and there are certainly many differences in their characters, a well-delivered speech as Helena will help the summer stock casting people to clearly visualize you as Hero.

If you looked through our guide and decided that you just loved Lady Macbeth and that you could conceivably play her (and who wouldn't want to play her?) that's terrific, but in the scenario I've given you (auditioning for sweet Hero), this choice wouldn't serve you well for this particular audition. Casting directors see a lot of actors in a short amount of time and need to be able to see you in the role they're casting quickly and easily. Help them to help you by choosing material that points the way.

Let's take a look at the second case I put forward; the instance where you're not auditioning to be considered for a particular role in a Shakespeare play, but are instead using your Shakespeare piece to show your work in general as an actor. This often happens in group auditions. *Group auditions are events where many different theatres are seeing many actors at the same time, cattle-call style, for a multitude of projects.* This is also a very common situation when you're auditioning for actor training programs. Let's say that you're auditioning for graduate training and have been asked to show a classical piece.

Chances are that the graduate program or programs you're auditioning for have asked to see "two contrasting monologues" and have specifically requested that one of those pieces be a classical piece. This is a very standard request for such programs. What do they mean, exactly, by a "contrasting monologue"? Isn't it contrasting enough that one of your pieces is a contemporary monologue and the other is classical?

Not really.

Contrasting monologues are really what they sound like. If your contemporary monologue is dramatic, find yourself a great piece in verse from one of Shakespeare's comedies, or a delightful piece from one of the romances. If your contemporary monologue is a comedic piece, chose a monologue with a heavier tone; look to Shakespeare's tragedies, histories, problem plays, or even a less lighthearted piece from one of the romances. Find a piece that shows another dimension of who you are as an actor.

"But wait!" you might be saying. "You helped me to understand the different categories of plays, the different types of characters that I could play, what kinds of pieces I might need to serve the requirements of a particular audition, but I don't have *time* to read through all of these plays right now to find the right material. My audition is in three weeks. I'm stressed and I need to figure this out quickly!"

I hear you. You have a life and other demands, and this needs to all come together super fast. In an ideal world—one in which you have ample time and mental space—the best thing to do would be to narrow down plays that you think have the right kinds of characters for you to play and to spend time really getting to know all of those possible plays. This is the best way.

But in the real world, sometimes we can't spend a lot of time with many different plays, so we need to cut corners. Here is how to cut corners in the selection process with integrity.

Here's where the Internet—which I cautioned you not to rely on as your Shakespeare text source—actually comes in handy. Once you've looked at the specific requirements of your audition, and once you've narrowed down some playable choices for your age and type from our chart in the previous chapter, you can go to a terrific online source called www.OpenSourceShakespeare.org. This resource will help you to look at all of the lines that the character that you are interested in speaks in the entire play! What a great way to see if he or she has a monologue that may interest you.

If you find a monologue or soliloquy that looks like a possible fit for you, then read a synopsis of the play. Does it sound even more interesting?

Once you've narrowed down your search in this way, then we will spend your limited time and energy wisely and really dig into the play you've chosen. This way of skimming texts that are unfamiliar to you is a great way to preview a lot of possibilities quickly. Often, your actor intuition will know very quickly which pieces have the possibility of connection for you and which ones will not. Go with your gut. Once your intuition has spoken and you've arrived at the piece you want to work on, you'll get down to business with the text itself.

7. Getting on Top of a Shakespeare Play Quickly

I have a confession to make to you—one that may shock you.

I have never read a Shakespeare play.

"Whoa . . . hold on!" you're probably saying. "You're a Shakespeare actor. And you teach acting Shakespeare at a university. And you coach Shakespeare productions. What do you mean you *never read* a Shakespeare play?"

Yes. It's true.

But I have a very good reason for this, and one that I'd like to share with you.

As we stated earlier, Shakespeare's plays were performed. They were written for actors on a stage, not readers in an armchair. So, if in Shakespeare's time, the plays were intended to be heard and not to be read, why should it be any different now?

When I was an undergraduate English literature major studying Shakespeare for the first time, I remember my fellow classmates struggling to read the assigned play for the week. They would sit in the library, usually distracted, often coming away with little understanding or command of what they'd just read.

While they were doing that, I would take my *Riverside Shakespeare* and sneak off to the library's "sound room." In the sound room, in exchange for your ID card, you could borrow a record, a record player and a giant pair of headphones for two hours (you can tell I'm old now, right?). I would open my *Riverside* to the play that I was studying and listen to the actors of the BBC perform the play in its entirety as I followed along in my book. The actors of the BBC brought the play to life for me each week. I came away with not only an intellectual understanding of the play, but a visceral and emotional connection to it.

I thought I was cheating.

It was easy and fun to learn the plays this way, and, I mean, anything that felt that fun and that easy had to be cheating, right?

Little did I know that this was not only a viable way to learn the plays, but it was the best way.

So here is my recommendation for you: listen to the play, don't read the play.

Things have changed a lot since my college days of listening to records in the university library on clunky headphones. These days there are complete versions of every play available to hear or watch online. Look at iTunes for audio and video recordings. Check out the Broadway Theatre Archive, a great resource for finding past productions of the plays to watch. Also check out a great website called Learn Out Loud: www.learnoutloud.com/Free-Online-Learning/Free-Video-Audio-Resources/Free-Shakespeare-Plays-on-Audio/315.

More and more possibilities are opening up all the time. But don't just listen to the text; have a well-edited version of the play in front of you. These two things—seeing the text and hearing it read—combine to make the best way and most enjoyable way to take command of the play.

Be a little bit cautious when watching Hollywood film versions of the plays, as many versions made into film are cut versions of the original text. Some are very faithful to the plays, but some take liberties and do a lot of chopping.

Don't listen to just one production of the play, listen to multiple versions. By listening to a few different productions with different interpretations, you are taking in many different possibilities for creating your character and their world. The one danger in listening to other actors' work is that, without even realizing it, you may be imitating or replicating their take on the character. My advice is not to spend too much time listening to any one actor's interpretation of your chosen piece, but to use recordings to get an overall feel for the play.

Another great tool as you explore your play? Invite your actor friends (or any of your classy, literate friends) over for drinks and read the play aloud. This is not only great fun, but a dynamic way to experience your chosen play.

Read some critical commentary if you can. Devote an hour to reading what scholars have said about your character and about your piece. You never know what ideas might unfold for you.

Experience your chosen play, and keep your mind open to all of the possibilities for interpretation of character. One actor's Hamlet is drastically different from another actor's Hamlet. Your version of your piece will ultimately be just that—your version. As doddering old Polonius said, surprisingly wisely, in *Hamlet,* "This above all: to thine own self be true."

8. Who Are You Talking To?

*M*y friend in New York is an opera teacher. He's been teaching studio voice for over forty years. He once told me that he says the same things over and over and over again to all of his singers. He joked, "One day I'm going to say, 'Sing ahh,' and then fall over dead from saying it so many times."

It's quite a visual.

Well, the acting teacher has a similar repeatable phrase—"Who are you talking to?"

Like "sing ahh," it's the first and most pertinent starting point for your work as an actor.

Why? Because you are always talking to someone when you're on stage. It's funny how all actors know this when they're doing a scene, and yet when actors go to auditions, they often go to this strange place that I call Monologue Land. Monologue Land is when it is not clear to the viewer who you are talking to and what you need from them. Needing something from somebody on stage is really, if you stop and think about it, the only reason to be on stage.

Which brings me to a question—what is the difference between a monologue and a soliloquy?

First let's talk about what monologues and soliloquies have in common. Both involve a solitary speaker. The difference between the monologue and the soliloquy is who is listening.

A "monologue"—from the Greek "monos" ("single") and "legein" ("to speak")—is a speech given by a single person to an audience (Harper 2014). *In a monologue, the listener or listeners may be the other characters on-stage. A monologue may also be directly addressed to the audience in the theatre.*

In a soliloquy, the speaker is alone and speaks to him- or herself on stage. The origin of this word says it all. It comes from the Latin *"solus"* ("alone") and *"loqui"* ("to speak")—to speak alone (Harper 2014). But a soliloquy is even more than speaking—really it is "thinking out loud." From a literary standpoint, the soliloquy is a way for the audience to understand what the character is thinking and feeling. This knowledge moves the play forward for the audience. But just as important, it's a way for the character to explore something of great importance within himself: he may attempt to untangle a problem, hatch a plan, propel himself to action, talk himself in or out of love, or come to a conclusion (good or bad) that will change him. Soliloquies are where big changes occur.

This distinction is a more than a semantic one for the actor. Knowing specifically *who* you are talking to is the most important thing when you're working on your piece.

Know to whom you are speaking, not generally, but in great detail. If I'm performing a monologue as Rosalind in the comedy *As You Like It* and I'm speaking to the character Phoebe (a lowly shepherdess), as the actor I should not only know, "Hey, I'm talking to Phoebe here," but I should know who *my* Phoebe is.

What does your Phoebe look like? What do her eyes look like? What texture is her hair? How does she laugh? How does she show disdain? How does she show delight? How does she hold her body? The more specifically you can picture who you are talking to, the more connected you will be to your imaginary partner and the greater your need on stage will be to change that person. General ideas lead to general acting. Specific visions create a captivating sense of reality on stage. Envision your Phoebe in great detail and see her on the back wall when you do your piece. That's not a speck of paint back there—that's Phoebe you're talking to!

What about the case of a monologue where you are talking to the audience? In the tragedy of *Othello*, the character Iago has an amazing monologue where he talks to the audience, telling them of his all-consuming hatred of Othello and laying out his plot for vengeance. Iago is figuring out the details of this plot in the moment and sharing it with everyone in the theatre.

The big mistake to make in this case, and the mistake actors often make, is to envision a generalized "audience." Well, remember that any audience is made up of specific people. The actor playing Iago has to envision a compelling need/objective for sharing his plot with them. Does he need to get the audience on his side and get them to see that he's justified in his hatred of Othello? Does he need the audience to recognize his brilliance and affirm and appreciate him? There are many possibilities. Whatever the actor decides is the most compelling reason to engage the audience, he has to envision specific audience members, not a generalized blob of an audience. He must see, "Ooo, that guy over there with the hat isn't buying it. I have to hit him with this next point," or, "That woman with the curly hair doesn't grasp that I'm serious. I have to scare her." If your piece dictates that you are speaking to the audience, find different points along the back wall of the audition room and imagine that there are different people there having different reactions to what you're saying. Specifically envision what they do, and how they look, and try to change their responses. And as you would in any audition situation, do not use the people in the room who are auditioning you unless you are specifically invited to do so, which is an occurrence more rare than the return of Halley's Comet. Involving those who are supposed to be watching your audition objectively puts them on the spot in an awkward way. They don't want to be your scene partner—they want to be free to sit back and watch you work.

What about the case of the soliloquy where you are talking to yourself on stage? The soliloquy is the most seemingly problematic of these three scenarios. Speaking to another character on stage is a fairly clear setup, and speaking to the audience provides you with clear targets for your action, but speaking to yourself on stage? How do you make that active?

Here's a way to think about it. Even when we talk to ourselves, we're talking to some kind of an audience for our thoughts. It may be that this audience for our thoughts is the divine. In Hamlet's famous soliloquy, "To be or not to be," he addresses the divine (here Shakespeare uses a literary device called an "apostrophe," *a direct appeal to the gods*). "Oh God, God, how weary, stale and unprofitable seem to me all the uses of this world," says Hamlet. If you think about it, when people are in great need of assistance or clarity, they turn to a divine force, however they envision that force. In this case a part of Hamlet's soliloquy is directed to the divine.

But there is another solution. And here's where I will turn from the divine to Bugs Bunny. Yes, you heard that right.

So, if you ever watched Bugs Bunny, you would know that there is this, well, this *thing* that happens in many episodes with Bugs. Bugs has this Angel Bunny with a halo and a harp on his one shoulder, looking angelic and dressed in white. On his other shoulder he has a red-clad Devil Bunny with horns and a pitchfork. If Bugs has a major dilemma, like debating whether or not he should he steal that carrot, Devil Bunny in all of his fire and brimstone hisses, "Go on, Bugs, take it. You know you want it," while Angel Bunny on her harp tells him all of the reasons why it would be wrong. And poor Bugs vacillates, going back and forth between the two powers inside his own head vying to be heard and wanting to win.

Well, Hamlet and Bugs Bunny have an awful lot in common. Inside of Hamlet's head in this play is the Devil Bunny Hamlet (in his case not exactly Devil Bunny Hamlet, but Manly Take Action Hamlet), who tells him to avenge his father's murder and to do it quickly, and the Angel Bunny Hamlet (in this case Reason-driven, Passive Hamlet), who counters expediency and action with due process, high morality, and logistics.

We do this when we talk to ourselves in real life (we all have soliloquies going on in our heads all of the time). If it's 1:00 a.m. and I'm going to the refrigerator to eat that last piece of cheesecake, a fun-loving-who-cares version of me is telling me that this is a perfectly great thing to do, and a disciplined, reasonable, responsible version of me is telling me this will make me fat and unhappy and give me high cholesterol. I address both of these versions of myself in my head as I make my decision whether or not to have my ill-chosen midnight snack.

This is what a soliloquy often is; the character flipping between this thought and that competing thought. The character puts forth a thesis statement, and then retracts it. They make a decision, and then they immediately overturn that decision. They happily barrel forward in one direction, only to stumble into a hidden truth within themselves. Once they uncover this truth, they become scared by the realization and they do a complete turnaround. Soliloquies are exciting things. When we are trying to change another person's thoughts, we often need to keep on a fairly logical and straightforward avenue of discourse. When we're talking to ourselves and in the process of changing our own thoughts, as we are in soliloquy, our brains can move at lightning speed.

When delivering your piece, a soliloquy, like a monologue, needs to be placed in the audition room outside of yourself. Even though the thoughts you speak are internal thoughts, they must not be turned inward on stage. Send your energy out to a specific target or targets, preferably along the back wall of the audition room, behind the auditioners' heads, just like you would with a monologue. Don't look up at the ceiling too much—the gods may be up there, but the auditioners ain't.

"But Laura, I'm talking to *myself*. I'm right here. I'm not on the back wall," you might say.

A version of yourself is out there on that back wall. See those different versions of your character that you speak to in your soliloquy. If you are Hamlet, speaking "To be or not to be," put Manly Take Action Hamlet out there in the audition room. See him. See what he looks like. Imagine how he responds. He is the version of your character that you will speak to when you are trying to "screw your courage to the sticking place" (okay, wrong play . . . Lady Macbeth said that). You'll address Manly Take Action Hamlet when you're trying to summon the gumption to commit suicide (the "or not to be" of the question). But in those moments of fear where you wonder what horrors would await you in the afterlife if you commit suicide (something that is against God's will), you will appeal to Reason-driven, Passive Hamlet. See him in a different spot on the back wall. The two versions of your character duke it out as the audience (the auditioners) watch. As you can imagine, converting your internally driven thoughts to an externally placed target or targets takes your piece from self-focused musings to an action-filled mental tug-of-war.

9. Your Given Circumstances

*W*e just talked about the ever-important question "Who are you talking to?" It's a vital question to ask, but this question goes hand in hand with other, equally important questions. You can't really know what you need from the person you're talking to without answering more about who you are, where you are, what your circumstances are, and what you need.

As for any acting piece, the playwright has given you information that you need to keep in mind as you prepare. This is all Acting 101, but it's amazing how often the basics go out the window when an actor encounters a classical piece. So let's take a few moments to go over the crucial pieces of information that you need to nail down in your head before tackling the other demands of your piece.

It may help you to write these answers down, either journal-style or by typing them out. It's so easy to cut corners as an actor (I know—I've done it, believe me). Making yourself write things out may help you to delve more deeply and thoroughly into the work so that nothing gets missed or glossed over. And you may or may not like to work this way, but I always think it's a good idea when speaking about your character to say, "I want this" or "I do this," instead of, "My character wants this" or "My character does this." You, of course, know that you are not Hamlet or Lady Macbeth or Iago, but speaking in the first person may help you get inside this other person's skin more easily.

GIVEN CIRCUMSTANCES QUESTIONS

Who Is Your Character?

In specific detail, what is your character's name, age, gender (and do they, in this monologue/soliloquy, appear as a gender other than what they truly are? Shakespeare was all about disguises and cross-dressing), social status (also, is their true social status revealed or disguised?), insecurities, hopes, pain, and aspirations? What do other people say about this character in the play? (Often what other people say about your character is your best way of getting information.)

In addition to this basic information that you would ask yourself to prepare any contemporary role, it may be useful to ask yourself about your character's humor.

The kind of humor I'm talking about here isn't about how funny your character is (although that is nice to know about, too). Rather, this is about the Renaissance concept of the four humors.

In Elizabethan times, it was believed that a person's physiological make-up —specifically the dominance of particular fluids in a person's body— dictated temperament and personality. If they had an overabundance of yellow bile in their body, for instance, they were said to be "choleric." They would often be rash, vengeful, and, as the Elizabethans would have said, "full of spleen." Our friend Prince Hamlet is said to be melancholic. He has too much black bile swirling around his royal Dane body; this is why he's such a bummer to be around. Knowing what your character's predominant humor is may give you a clearer picture of what drives him, how he carries himself, and how he deals with the world.

Shakespeare often spoke of the humors in his writing. Chances are, mention is made of your character's humor in the play, either by him- or herself or by another character.

Below is a listing of the four humors and the effect on personality that each was believed to have had.

Humor	Sanguine	Choleric	Phlegmatic	Melancholic
Body substance	blood	yellow bile	phlegm	black bile
Produced by	liver	spleen	lungs	gall bladder
Element	air	fire	water	earth
Qualities	hot and moist	hot and dry	cold and moist	cold and dry
Complexion and Body type	red-cheeked, corpulent	red-haired, thin	corpulent	sallow, thin
Personality	amorous, happy, generous, optimistic, irresponsible	violent, vengeful, short-tempered, ambitious	sluggish, pallid, cowardly	introspective, sentimental, gluttonous

(Adapted from Kazlev 2004)

What Is the Current Situation?

What's going on at this point in the play? What's the problem that needs to be overcome? What, in a nutshell, is your character's predicament right now?

Where Are They?

Literally, physically, what kind of a space is your character in? What country are they in? Are they in a literal or a mythic world? Are they in a prison, are they in a bedchamber, are they in a court, are they in a town square, or are they in a forest? Your character's location will affect their behavior. Is it sunny? Raining? Damp? How does this affect them?

When Is This Event Taking Place?

What season is it? What time of day or night is it? The energy your character feels alone at midnight is different than the kind of energy she feels in the morning.

Why Is This Event Happening Right Now?

This is what I call "The Passover Question." On the Jewish holiday Passover, as part of the reading of the Haggadah, the question is asked, "Why is this night different from all other nights?" Ask the same question about your piece. Why is this moment in the play different from all other moments? Why is this event happening right now? Why didn't this particular thing happen last year or five years ago, or five minutes ago, or yesterday or tomorrow? What happened that makes this moment in time unique and demands that this needs to happen right now?

THE MOMENT BEFORE

The moment before any scene begins on stage, something happened.

Scenes don't begin in a vacuum. Your character experienced something that prompts the next moment, even if the audience doesn't see it. Monologues and soliloquies should not begin in a vacuum either. Before your character speaks their monologue or soliloquy, something just happened to them: this is what is known as "the moment before."

Before Viola in *Twelfth Night* speaks her soliloquy, "I left no ring with her: what means this lady?" the Countess Olivia's servant, Malvolio, follows Viola (who in this part of the play is disguised as a boy page, Cesario) down the street. Ostensibly Malvolio is returning a ring that that "Cesario" left with Countess Olivia. Poor confused Viola left no such ring with Olivia and has not yet fully caught on to the fact that it is Olivia's ploy to see the (she thinks!) young man again. The moment before Viola's soliloquy is the moment when charmless, curmudgeonly Malvolio throws the ring to the ground, chastising her, as a confused Viola struggles to figure out just what the heck is going on. The actor who is playing Viola in an audition situation needs to envision this moment so that she starts the piece in a proper state of bewilderment, horror, and fascination, as the piece demands.

In this case, Shakespeare very clearly spelled out the moment before for the actor. It is right there in the scene prior to Malvolio's exit. We know exactly what just happened to Viola. Sometimes, however, the moment before is not clearly defined in the script and the actor has to make their own determination about what just happened. Before Hamlet speaks the soliloquy "To be or not to be," we cannot be one hundred percent certain what he was doing. The scene prior to this soliloquy involves Claudius, Polonius, Gertrude, and Ophelia. Hamlet enters to speak the soliloquy from off stage. In this case, the actor needs to decide for himself exactly what Hamlet was doing before coming on stage, and exactly where he came from.

Why is all of this important? Because so many times I see an actor at an audition "just start"; that is, they introduce themselves and their piece, and then a hot second later they're off and running, doing their monologue or soliloquy. There is no moment of grounding, no establishment of place or situation. So, before you start your piece, take a moment. Ground yourself. Feel your feet planted on the ground. Think about what just happened to your character: what someone just said to you, what they did, how they left you. Think about where you came from and where you were going. See the space. Know exactly what just occurred and what you think about it. Then and only then should you start to speak. I guarantee you, if you take five seconds to do this, it will set your work apart from the herds of actors who forget this important step.

THE CHARACTER'S OBJECTIVE AND THE STAKES

The objective is what the character needs to get from another character or characters on stage. No one is ever just on stage talking. Your character is always working to get something. An objective (or goal) is the specific thing that your character is striving to get at this moment, from someone else or from himself or herself. It has to be incredibly important that they achieve this goal. What they need has to matter.

The problem that I often see with monologues and soliloquies is that I am not sure, as the audience, what it is that the character really *wants*. I often see a whole lot of talking but no clear need. As an audience, we want to see people on stage needing things. This is what makes us care about them. Without a clear need, your character has no reason to be on stage speaking.

So take a good hard look at the play. Ask yourself, "What do I (the character) want in this play?" An even better way to ask the question is, "What am I fighting for?"

Once you figure out what you're fighting for in the play, the next step is to ask yourself what you're fighting for in the specific scene that contains your monologue.

Let's look at the play *Macbeth* (or "The Scottish Play," if you're saying the name aloud in a theatre). If I look at Lady Macbeth's objective in the play as a whole (her "superobjective" is what we will call it), it is to help Macbeth to become king so that she can become queen. She's fighting to get Macbeth onto the throne. It's a matter of life or death for her.

Let's say that I'm working on Lady Macbeth's monologue from Act 1, scene 7, "Was the hope drunk Wherein you dressed yourself?" In this speech Lady M realizes that Macbeth is questioning his own motives and having second thoughts about killing Duncan (the next step in their plan to seize the throne). I can look at this scene and realize that Lady M is worried that Macbeth is starting to act like a weenie, and she's deeply concerned that he may be starting to veer away from their ambitious goal. Her objective in the scene, therefore, is to get Macbeth to "man up" in order for him to continue with their plans.

Every choice that I make as an actor delivering this monologue will be shaped by knowing that my goal—the thing that I desperately need—is to get Macbeth to man up. Take a look at the monologue and see how this clear need drives through the text:

> Was the hope drunk
> Wherein you dress'd yourself? Hath it slept since?
> And wakes it now to look so green and pale
> At what it did so freely? From this time
> Such I account thy love. Art thou afeard
> To be the same in thine own act and valor
> As thou art in desire? Wouldst thou have that
> Which thou esteem'st the ornament of life,
> And live a coward in thine own esteem,
> Letting "I dare not" wait upon "I would,"
> Like the poor cat I' th' adage?
>   What beast was 't, then,
> That made you break this enterprise to me?
> When you durst do it, then you were a man;

I am fighting to get through to Macbeth. I see him clearly in my head. I know what I want.

I also have to know what the consequences will be if I *don't* get what I want. This is called the "stakes" of the piece. *The stakes are what is at risk for the character if he or she loses.* Ask yourself, "What is the consequence if I don't get what I want?" Make it life or death. "If I don't get to be the queen, I will die." If you are Lady Olivia in *Twelfth Night*: "If I don't get Cesario to love me, I will stay in mourning for my whole life." Make it as important as you possibly can to achieve your objective. The consequence of not getting what you want needs to be very high in order for the scene to be interesting.

When you know who you are talking to, when you know what you desperately need from them, and when you know clearly what will happen to you if you don't get what you need, the piece practically acts itself, doesn't it?

CONFLICT AND THE CHARACTER'S OBSTACLE

Oh, but life would be too easy if we knew what we wanted, went after it with gusto, and we got it. In plays, just like in life, things always stand in the way of getting what we want.

In every scene in every play, there is an obstacle. *The obstacle is the thing preventing you, the character, from achieving your objective and getting what you want.*

The obstacle provides the conflict in the scene.

Let's look at it another way:

- I want to get "A" in the scene.
- "B" is in my way and preventing me from getting "A."
- Conflict arises because "B" is blocking me from getting "A," and I am not getting what I am fighting for.

So conflict comes from having an obstacle in the way of getting what you want. But what is conflict on stage? The best way to define "conflict" is *"when two opposing forces collide."* We've all experienced conflicts in our lives. Conflicts arise when different people fight for opposing things and sparks fly as each tries to win. While conflict may be something we desperately try to avoid in life (depending on your personality type), conflict is the stuff that theatre is made of. If there is no conflict, there is no play! Conflict is the basis of all theatre.

Conflict is clear and easy to see when we have two or more characters on stage. But what about conflict in the case of monologues and soliloquies? Where do we see conflict when it is just you, the lone actor, up there on the stage?

Oh, but you see? You're not alone. You're talking to someone, whether that someone is your imaginary partner or an aspect of yourself that you're trying to change.

This is why it's so important that you clearly envision the person you're talking to. How do they react to what you say? What is their response?

Clearly see what the imaginary person you're speaking to is doing as you speak to them. Do they roll their eyes at you? Do they walk away? Do they put up their sword? Do they plug their ears? What kind of an obstacle are they throwing in your way to prevent you from getting through to them? Picture what they are doing. Make it specific.

What about a soliloquy? In the soliloquy, you are your own obstacle. The conflict is a conflict within yourself, a battle between the different parts of your mind that are vying for control. To help you play the conflict in a soliloquy, it may help you to name the opposing forces in your psyche. Is it Moral Macbeth vs. Ambitious Macbeth? Is it Loving Othello vs. Jealous Othello? Name the players in the conflict. When does each surface? Who is winning? Who is losing? Every few lines, write down who is winning and who is losing. How often does it change?

Identify the obstacle and find the conflict. See the person you are talking to clearly. Identify wins and losses. If you find the conflict, you'll find the electric charge in your piece.

TACTICS AND BEAT SHIFTS

Once you know what your character wants and needs (what your objective is), and once you identify what the obstacle is that prevents you from getting what you want, you need to figure out by what means you're going to try to *get* what you want.

These are your character's "tactics."

Tactics are the specific things that a character does to get what he or she needs from another character. (You may hear other theatre teachers refer to these as "actions"—both are good terms.)

It's like this; when we want something really badly, we find different ways of trying to get what we want. When one thing we're doing isn't getting us closer to winning our goal, we change our approach so that we have a better chance of getting what we want from the other person.

Think about the last conversation you had where you really needed something from the person you were talking to. When you could see that what you were doing wasn't getting you anywhere, what did you do? I bet you didn't keep on doing the thing that wasn't working! I bet you regrouped and reworked your approach, and that you kept doing this until you felt like you were getting somewhere.

As an example of how to play a tactic, let's look at an everyday example for a teacher like me; a student wants to get an extension on a paper assignment (oh, I see this one a lot . . .).

> *The situation:* Student A had too much on her plate at school to write her paper.
>
> *Her objective?* To get me to give her a three-day extension on a term paper.
>
> *Her beginning tactic:* to make me feel sympathetic.
>
> Student A tells me that she has some stressful things going

on with her family, as well as roommate drama and an upcoming housing move. When she realizes that trying to make me feel sympathetic to her case isn't really working and that she's no closer to getting me to change her paper due date, she knows she needs to change her tactic.

Her next tactic: To make me feel guilty.

Student A tells me that she has more work for my class than for any of her other classes and that my paper deadlines are too close together. No other professor heaps on the work like I do. When she realizes that this tactic is not getting her any closer to her objective (getting me to change her paper due date)–in fact, it is backfiring on her and making me feel defensive–she knows she needs to change her tactic again.

Her next tactic? To make me feel valuable.

Student A does a turnaround and tells me that she just respects me so much and loves my class so much that she just really doesn't want to do a half-assed job on her paper—the work really matters to her and my opinion matters too. Since I am an actor and I like constant praise and reassurance, her third tactic—to make me feel valuable—works. Student A gets an extension until Tuesday.

Student A wins her objective.

Notice that in each case we framed the tactic in terms of how Student A was trying to make *me* feel. How *she* was feeling wasn't the important thing. The important thing is how she was affecting *my* feelings. Making me feel sympathetic didn't work. Making me feel guilty didn't work, but finally, making me feel valuable did work.

So Shakespeare, of course, writes more interesting material than the "Give me a paper extension" scene that I just made up, but hopefully you can see where I'm going with this.

In your scene (and you need to start thinking about your monologue or soliloquy as a scene, because really, that's what it is), you need to change tactics and change them often!

When a scene or a monologue is boring, it's because the actor isn't switching up their tactics enough. The work becomes stagnant and one-note, and the audience checks out. Look at a great Shakespeare actor like Kenneth Branagh or Patrick Stewart. They change tactics on practically every line. Watch their work and look for this in their scenes. Name for yourself the tactics that they're using. It's a fun game, and it will show you how some great Shakespeare acting takes shape!

Let's take another look at Lady M's monologue:

> Was the hope drunk
> Wherein you dress'd yourself? Hath it slept since?
> And wakes it now to look so green and pale
> At what it did so freely? From this time
> Such I account thy love. Art thou afeard
> To be the same in thine own act and valor
> As thou art in desire? Wouldst thou have that
> Which thou esteem'st the ornament of life,
> And live a coward in thine own esteem,
> Letting "I dare not" wait upon "I would,"
> Like the poor cat i' th' adage?

Often when this piece is done it is all one note. It is so easy for the actor to play one tactic and only one tactic; make Macbeth feel like a wimp. While this certainly is a tactic to play in the piece, if it is the only tactic that you use, things get boring really quickly, right?

What else can you do here? Making him feel like a weenie will get you only so far. Do too much of that and old Mackers starts to tune out. He doesn't want to hear criticism. He blocks you out–"la la la"–plugging his ears to your womanly chastisements. What would happen if you were to switch your tactic to "make him feel sexy" (around the lines where you talk about "Art thou afeard to be the same in thine own act and valor" part). Yes! That's getting his attention! Now he's listening to you! He's getting a little turned on by this talk of his desire. Now he's feeling like a man (that's your objective, right? To get him to "man up"?). Ooooh! But now that he's listening to you and feeling a little more manly, switch it up again! Make him feel empowered around the lines "Letting 'I dare not' wait upon 'I would' like the poor cat i' th' adage."

Read the piece over to yourself using the tactics as I outlined them so far:

Lady M

> Was the hope drunk   *Make Macbeth feel ashamed*
> Wherein you dress'd yourself? Hath it slept since?
> And wakes it now to look so green and pale
> At what it did so freely? From this time

Such I account thy love.
                    Art thou afeard | *Make Macbeth feel sexy* |
To be the same in thine own act and valor
As thou art in desire?
                    Wouldst thou have that | *Make Macbeth feel empowered* |
Which thou esteem'st the ornament of life,
And live a coward in thine own esteem,
Letting "I dare not" wait upon "I would,"
Like the poor cat i' th' adage?

So far, so good! We're really mixing things up here and trying to get Macbeth to man up in different ways. It seems like maybe it's starting to work a little . . .

Then Macbeth says:

                    Prithee, peace:
I dare do all that may become a man;
Who dares do more is none.

Even though you are alone on stage and this is a monologue, listen to what Macbeth says in your head. How does he say it? Is he continuing on with the sexy, empowered thing? Is he playing sexy-time back and showing you that he really *is* a man, or is he not buying what you're doing and shutting you down? Make a choice in your mind about what he's doing.

Finish up your monologue with an unexpected tactical switch:

Lady M
                    What beast was 't, then,
That made you break this enterprise to me? | *Make Macbeth feel disgusting* |
When you durst do it, then you were a man;
And to be more than what you were, you would
Be so much more the man.

Wow! Either way you decide in your head to hear Macbeth's line—whether it is playing along with the hot game or putting you in your place, this tactical switchup stings! It yanks Macbeth off of the path he was on and cuts him down, and it makes your audience wake up and pay attention!

This is just one small example. There are endless possibilities.

I hope that this example helps you to see these things:

- Switching up your tactics often in your monologue makes things very, very interesting.

- The most obvious choice (in this case making him feel like poo) isn't always the most interesting choice. Dig deeper and look at all of the possibilities.
- Envisioning what the other character says to you and how they, in turn, are trying to make *you* feel makes your monologue a compelling and active scene.

Do you see how much fun this can be? And you thought auditions were scary.

A Paperwork Checklist

Here is a quick recap of what we just talked about. I find it helpful to have a checklist of important questions to work from every time I tackle a new monologue or soliloquy (or revisit an old one). Write down these answers for yourself. Make extra copies of your soliloquy/monologue to mark up!

- *Given circumstances questions:*
  - Who is your character (in detail)? What is your character's humor?
  - What is the current situation?
  - Where are you? What country and what specific place? How does this place make you feel?
  - When is this event taking place?
  - Why is this event happening right now?
- *Who are you talking to?* What, in detail, do they look like?
- *Objective:* What do you want from the person you are talking to? What are you fighting for?
- *Stakes:* What bad thing is going to happen if you don't get what you want?
- *Moment before:* What happened the moment before the monologue/soliloquy began?
- *Obstacle:* What is in the way of getting what you want?
- *Conflict:* What is the conflict?
- *Tactics:* Write out how you are going to try to work the other person over to get what you want. What are you going to do to them? How are you going to try to make them feel? (Write these tactics down on your monologue/soliloquy next to your text).
- *Images:* Shakespeare's language is a landscape painted in words. Learn to see, smell, and taste the images and your audience will do the same.

○ Identify the images present in your monologue and list them.
○ Look up the definitions of the words as Shakespeare used them. Then rewrite them in your own words.
○ Describe in a sentence or two how each of these images makes you feel. What do you see? Use sensory descriptions for yourself: what does this image look like, feel like, taste like, smell like? The more specifically you identify it, the more specifically you will paint the picture for your audience. Help them to see what you see.

10. The Very Special Case
of the Histories

*I*f you choose to work on a monologue or soliloquy from one of Shakespeare's histories, there are a few more questions that you might want to ask yourself.

We talked in the Finding Your Match section about the importance of knowing a little bit about the events behind your history! So, in addition to the checklist of regular questions that we just went through, there are a few more things to think about. Why? Because unlike many of the comedies or romances that Shakespeare wrote (which may have been inspired by real events or previously told stories, but were meant to be taken as fictions), Shakespeare's history plays are intended to represent real historical events. Granted, the portrayal of these events might be rather colored by Shakespeare's own prejudices or the prejudices of the patrons that he was trying to flatter by writing them (remember, playwrights needed to curry favor with kings, queens, and other wealthy and powerful patrons to keep themselves in a job and out of trouble, so bear in mind that the histories were often written in a way that supported or flattered certain key political players in their telling). Nevertheless, there is some historical information you'll want to know in order to give monologues or soliloquies from the histories your best shot.

My colleague David Meldman, self-described "Shakespeare Übermensch," generated this list of questions to ask yourself when you tackle a history play. If you're pressed for time, you may not be able to delve as deeply as you might like into these questions, but even beginning to think along these lines may help you to a deeper and more informed and compelling audition. You can always come back to do greater research another day, since hopefully the history piece that you've chosen will be a keeper long past this particular audition!

Some Questions That May Help You When Working on Shakespeare's Histories

Many of Shakespeare's histories concern various wars among noble houses for control of England's throne. These conflicts were similar to national-scale gang warfare. Who you were loyal to and why, what "colors" you wore, determined much of your fate. Developing a full understanding of who you are, where you come from, and what you fight for is central to inhabiting the world of the play, and these were second-nature matters of identity in Shakespeare's time.

You will likely need to do outside research on the historical figures represented in the plays, as well as analysis of the play itself (Shakespeare took many dramatic liberties, but many insights can be had and many questions clarified from actual history).

- What is the central conflict, and who is it between?
- Which side are you on?
- What is your class level, and how does this inform your goals? (are you a commoner, middle-class, noble, prince/princess, king/queen?)
- What is your family affiliation? Supply a small genealogy mapping your relationship to the other characters in the play. If you are "independent," map your relationships/loyalties.
- What do you, personally, stand to gain if your side wins? (The throne itself? A higher position? Honor and glory?)
- What do you stand to lose?
- Before the central conflict, what were your relationships like to the other powers/houses/or characters in the play? Why did this change?
- Describe your religious background and how it informs your objectives, obstacles, and relationships. For example, are you a devout Catholic, Protestant, or another religion? Do you aspire to heavenly virtue, or do you relish earthly indulgence? Does your faith give you comfort, or create conflict? Do you seek to appease or defy the deities? Why?

11. Digging into Your Piece: Meter, Inflection, and Images

*B*y now you've already done a lot of work. You've selected your piece, you've watched the play, and you've asked yourself some really important questions about the text. It is time to start to move toward speaking your piece!

POETIC METER (AND YOUR NEW BUDDY, MR. IAMB)

Just as a piece of music is made up of measures and individual notes, we can break verse down into smaller units to see how it is constructed.

The simplest building block of verse for Shakespeare is called the *iamb* (pronounced like "I am").

An iamb is a metrical unit, or foot of verse, that has one unstressed syllable followed by one stressed syllable.

If we were to notate an iamb, it would look like this: ◡ /
Where ◡ is the unstressed syllable of the word
and / is the stressed syllable of the word.

Let's find an example word to illustrate what an iamb is. Let's look at the word *upon*.

We can see that that word *upon* has two syllables, where "uh" is unstressed and "PON" is stressed.

If we were to map out the word *upon* as an iamb, it would look like this:

$$◡ \; /$$
upon

Speak the word aloud. Do you feel how all of the weight and strength of the word is on the "PON" part and the "uh" is just like a little launch pad to the "PON"? "uhPON"?

So, this little modest thing—an unstressed beat followed by a stressed beat—is a single metrical foot and the building block of all Shakespeare's verse. That's all there is to Mr. Iamb. He's very popular, but also very humble.

But Mr. Iamb doesn't like to travel alone. He likes to hit the road with friends.

Did you ever hear the term *iambic pentameter*? Iambic pentameter is when five iambs get together to form a line of verse ("pent" meaning five, and "meter" meaning, well, meter). Shakespeare wrote the majority of his verse in iambic pentameter.

A line of iambic pentameter (five iambs in a row) would look like this:

$$\smile / \mid \quad \smile / \mid \quad \smile / \mid \quad \smile / \mid \quad \smile /$$

Check it out. Five iambs, all in a row!

The big bold vertical line that you see between the iambs is drawn to separate out the metrical feet. It's a good to do this so you can count how many metrical feet make up a line of text. More on that in a bit . . .

Let's find an example sentence from Shakespeare to illustrate what a line of iambic pentameter looks like. How about this line from *A Midsummer Night's Dream*, spoken by Helena?

"How happy some o'er other some can be!"

If I were to map this out in iambic pentameter, it would look like this:

$$\smile \quad / \quad \smile \quad / \quad \smile \quad / \quad \smile \quad / \quad \smile \quad /$$
How ha|ppy some| o'er oth|er some| can be!

It would sound a little like this if you read it:

How HAppy SOME o'er OTHer SOME can BE!

Five metrical feet (five iambs in a row) make up the line of the text. And do you see how sometimes two different iambs share the same word (for instance, the word "HAppy" is split between two different metrical feet; in effect, it straddles two iambs).

Let's look at a few more lines of this speech in the same way:

How happy some o'er other some can be!
Through Athens I am thought as fair as she.
But what of that? Demetrius thinks not so;
He will not know what all but he do know;

Maps out to look like this:

$$\smile \quad / \quad \smile \quad / \quad \smile \quad / \quad \smile \quad / \quad \smile \quad /$$
How ha|ppy some| o'er oth|er some| can be!

$$\smile \quad / \quad \smile \quad / \quad \smile \quad / \quad \smile \quad / \quad \smile \quad /$$
Through Ath|ens I| am thought| as fair |as she.

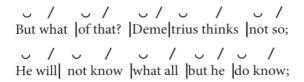

But what |of that? |Deme|trius thinks |not so;

He will| not know |what all |but he |do know;

Read it aloud, following the unstressed and stressed marks.
It should sound kind of like this:

> How HAppy SOME o'er OTHer SOME can BE!
> Through ATHens I am THOUGHT as FAIR as SHE.
> But WHAT of THAT? DeMEtruis THINKS not SO;
> He WILL not KNOW what ALL but HE do KNOW;

Other Meters

It is important for you to know that Shakespeare did not only write in iambic pentameter. Certain lines of his texts, or even whole little chunks of his texts, often appear in other kind of meters.

Here are other kinds of iambic verse. In addition to iambic pentameter there is:

iambic hexameter (6 metrical feet) $\cup/$ |$\cup/$ |$\cup/$ |$\cup/$ |$\cup/$ |$\cup/$

iambic tetrameter (4 metrical feet) $\cup/$ |$\cup/$ |$\cup/$ |$\cup/$

iambic trimeter (3 metrical feet) $\cup/$ |$\cup/$ |$\cup/$

iambic dimeter (2 metrical feet) $\cup/$ |$\cup/$

In your soliloquy you are most likely to encounter pentameter, but sometimes you may find hexameter or tetrameter. What is interesting is that Shakespeare's use of different iambic meters is no accident! Some of Shakespeare's characters in *A Midsummer Night's Dream*, for example, speak primarily in tetrameter. Inhabitants of the fairy world like Puck speak differently than other characters in the play. Shakespeare uses a different rhythm to signify that these characters are from a different world. The witches in *Macbeth* also speak a lot of tetrameter. Think about the famous words "double, double, toil and trouble/ fire burn and cauldron bubble." Their speech in this four-footed rhythm has the quality of an incantation. Not only is it in four metrical feet (tetrameter) rather than the pentameter of most of the rest of the play, but the feet are inverted! They start on a stressed syllable rather than an unstressed syllable (in very particular kind of meter called "trochaic tetrameter," in case you want to impress people at parties . . .). Shakespeare uses this different kind of poetic meter deliberately to say to the viewer, "Hey, viewer! We're not in Kansas anymore! These chicks are weird! See? They don't speak like everybody else. You better watch out for them! Everything in their world is upside down, including the meter!"

You may also be working on a soliloquy or monologue where the text is predominantly in pentameter but has a line of hexameter thrown in here and there. The piece can then, after a line of hexameter, switch back into pentameter for a few lines, and then back into hexameter again. This switch in meter can be significant; it can show that your character's thoughts are speeding up or changing direction. It may indicate that your character has too much joy or dread to be contained in the framework of pentameter. It may be that your character is uncovering a truth or coming to a realization. Or, in the case of our friend Hamlet, it just may be that he has too darn much to say to fit into pentameter. Whatever the cause or case, Shakespeare used changes in meter to say something about your character or about your character's frame of mind or thought process. For the actor, a switchup in meter can be a huge acting clue! So if you see that your meter is shifting, pay attention.

Crazy Little Thing Called Scansion

Let's go back to Mr. Iamb. Whether he's making up pentameter, hexameter, tetrameter, knowing how he works and being able to feel his down-up/unstressed-stressed pulse is going to really help your acting. We're going to look at some basic tools to start to map out the rhythmic pulses in your text. Figuring out the rhythmic structure of your text has a name. It is called "scansion." Quite simply, *scansion is scanning a piece of text to understand how it is rhythmically constructed*. The way that we just notated Helena's speech in *A Midsummer Night's Dream* is scansion. Easy, right?

Understanding the rhythmic underpinnings of your text is no mere intellectual exercise. By identifying the rhythmic pulse of Shakespeare's language, you as the actor can find a visceral connection to its heart.

The problem with way that many actors speak Shakespeare text is that they ignore the pulse of the language. They ride over the top of the language or work against it, rather than finding a way to connect with it and let the words take them on a ride. Scansion is the way to find that beating pulse.

Actors speaking Shakespeare texts often make intellectual decisions about how to speak the language. "I'm going to stress this word right here because I think that it is important!" they might say. Or (worse yet) they say, "I just intuitively know which words to stress." When working on a *contemporary* text, actors *do* have to decide which words are the most important words and which words to stress. This is called "choosing the operative word." But guess what? Shakespeare and his poetry actually do this work *for* us! And if we do some scansion, all of those important words that we need to stress just pop right on out without us having to think about it and without us getting in the way of it all and mucking it up!

When you do your scansion and follow the natural stresses that appear in the lines, the meaning emerges. Let's look at this example from *Macbeth* again:

> If it were done, when 'tis done, then 'twere well
> It were done quickly. If th' assassination
> Could trammel up the consequence, and catch
> With his surcease, success; that but this blow
> Might be the be-all and the end-all—here,
> But here, upon this bank and [shoal] of time,
> We'ld jump the life to come.

Let's just look at those first two lines. Actors who don't do their scansion usually say the lines like this (I'll capitalize the stresses):

> If IT were DONE when tis DONE then 'twere WELL
> it were DONE QUICKly.

Yeah. We kind of get what Macbeth is saying. Kind of . . .

Let's do the same thing that we did for Helena's *Midsummer Night's Dream* text; scansion.

Look at what happens when you do the scansion on the lines. The exquisite logic of this though emerges without your effort.

> ◡ / ◡ / ◡ / ◡ / ◡ /
> If it |were done| when 'tis |done then| 'twere well

> ◡ / ◡ / ◡
> It were |done quickly

> If IT were DONE when TIS done THEN 'twere WELL
> It WERE done QUICKly.

Do you see how the meaning just comes out? Macbeth is saying, "Oh, boy, if this thing truly needs to happen (killing the king), then when it's over it had better really be over, and if I'm gonna do this, I guess I'd better do it fast." The meaning is crystal clear when you follow the pulse of the scansion. But if you put the stress of the line in a slightly misplaced spot, this tight logical sequence falls apart. Good job, scansion! Thanks a bunch! Do you see? Shakespeare, who is probably smarter than the smartest of us all, did the thinking for us. Apply the tool, and Shakespeare's logic is revealed.

So, in addition to uncovering the true meaning of the text (a pretty darn important thing), when we follow the scansion it also makes Shakespeare . . . well, it makes Shakespeare sound like *Shakespeare*!

To illustrate what I mean, let's jump back to the *Midsummer* example for a minute. Speak aloud these lines, following the scansion:

> ⌣ / ⌣ / ⌣ / ⌣ / ⌣ /
> How **ha**|ppy **some**| o'er **oth**|er **some**| can **be**!

> ⌣ / ⌣ / ⌣ / ⌣ / ⌣ /
> Through **Ath**|ens **I**| am **thought**| as **fair** |as **she**.

> ⌣ / ⌣ / ⌣ / ⌣ / ⌣ /
> But **what** |of **that**? |**Deme**|trius **thinks** |not **so**;

> ⌣ / ⌣ / ⌣ / ⌣ / ⌣ /
> He **will**| not **know** |what **all** |but **he** |do **know**;

What happens when you hit those stressed syllables with gusto, and let the unstressed syllables simply carry you to the next stress? It starts to sound a little more like music, doesn't it? Think of it a little less like speech and a little more like singing.

Do you see how hitting what is stressed, and letting what is unstressed kind of float away, carries you through the line of text? The text starts to lift you and drive you forward. It flows, it is lifted, and it is heightened.

Sing Your Scansion

You can even do a really fun thing to help you to discover this and actually sing the text. Chose two pitches comfortably in your singing range: make the lower note the unstressed part of the syllable, and the higher note the stressed part of the syllable. Sing your scansion! If you like to sing, this can really help you to feel the difference between what is stressed and what is unstressed.

In addition to finding the pulse of the language, mapping out the verse also helps you to see how things are pronounced. Look at the name "Demetrius" in the text. We would think that this name would have four syllables and be pronounced . . . Duh-MEET-ree-us.

Well, if we pronounce all four of those syllables in this line of poetry (Duh-MEET-ree-us) we wind up with an extra syllable in this very nicely balanced speech where everything fits so well into iambic pentameter.

But if we shorten the name to be pronounced with three syllables instead . . .

Duh-MEET-rus, then the name fits beautifully into the line of iambic pentameter verse with no disruptions in the music.

⌣ / ⌣ / ⌣ / ⌣ / ⌣ /
But what |of that? |**Deme**|**trius** thinks |not so;

This may seem like a minor thing, but believe me. When actors do not know how many syllables a word in Shakespeare's text should be given, the meter goes wonky. Make too many words in his text too long (or too short, for that matter) and the verse starts to fall apart and not sound like verse anymore. Figure out how the words all fit into the framework of the verse, and you flow with the music of the poetry rather than disrupting it!

Mr. Iamb's Friends: Trochee, Spondee, and Company

Many times you are doing your scansion and everything is going along swimmingly using iamb after iamb in nice, neat iambic pentameter . . . but then you come to a place where those iambs just don't fit or feel right. It is like the music stops and the record scratches. What gives?

Well, when that happens to you, chances are that an iamb doesn't fit quite right in that particular line of poetry. You see, although the iamb is the building block of Shakespeare's verse construction, other kinds of metrical feet sometimes make up the text. So, when something feels like it doesn't fit right, instead of using Mr. Iamb in one of those metrical feet, you may need use one of his good friends instead.

So let's introduce you to Mr. Iamb's good friends. They are:

trochee	/⌣	stressed, unstressed
spondee	//	streesed, stressed
pyrrhic	⌣⌣	unstressed, unstressed
anapest	⌣⌣/	unstressed, unstressed, stressed
dactyl	/⌣⌣	stressed, unstressed, unstressed
amphibrach	⌣/⌣	unstressed, stressed, unstressed
amphimacer	/⌣/	stressed, unstressed, stressed

Don't get too hung up on names. The important thing for you to know is that sometimes an iamb just doesn't cut it and you need to employ another kind of metrical foot as you map out your text. And no . . . you are not imagining things. Sometimes metrical feet can have three syllables instead of two.

Let's look at a few examples. Here is a piece of the prologue to *The Life of Henry the Fifth*:

> Think, when we talk of horses, that you see them
> Printing their proud hooves i' th' receiving earth;
> For 'tis your thoughts that now must deck our kings,

Uh-oh. Things are weird already! When you go to scan that first line, no matter how many times you play with it, you'll find that you have no choice but to put an extra unstressed beat at the end of the line:

$$\smile \quad / \quad \smile \quad / \quad \smile \quad / \quad \smile \quad / \quad \smile \quad / \quad \smile$$
Think, when| we talk |of hor|ses, that |**you see them**

Do you remember how with the name "Demetrius" we found a cool way to shorten the name so that we could keep the poetry in iambic pentameter? Well, sometimes there's nothing we can do to shorten anything, and we wind up with an extra unstressed beat that we just can't do much of anything about. We need that extra beat; there's no getting rid of it. We're stuck with it.

In such cases we wind up with something called a "feminine ending." *A feminine ending is an extra, unstressed beat at the end the line of verse.*

Feminine endings are fun because they are an extra little beat to play with in your text. We may want to look at that extra unstressed beat as a little springboard into the next line, or it could even do the opposite in some cases–it might serve as a way for us to slow down as we feel the energy of that extra unstressed beat.

Sometimes (especially when punctuation appears in the middle of the line, or we don't really feel right separating a multisyllabic word), we can move that extra unstressed beat into the center of the line. In this case, it is something called an *epic caesura* (*epic* meaning "big" and *caesura* meaning "pause"). *An epic caesura is simply an extra, unstressed beat that causes you to pause in the middle of a line.*

So, back to our line in question:

$$\smile \quad / \quad \smile \quad / \quad \smile \quad / \quad \smile \quad / \quad \smile \quad / \quad \smile$$
Think, when| we talk |of hor|ses, that |**you see them**

You can see that we have a feminine ending on our hands in that fifth metrical foot! And what is this three-syllable foot ("you see them") that I just scanned called? Which of Mr. Iamb's friends is this? Why, it's his good friend *amphimacer* to the rescue!

But now I bet when we look at the next line of the text, we'll return to regular old iambic pentameter and all will be well right?

Nope! Things continue to be a little weird with this text. Let's look at:

Printing their proud hooves i' th' receiving earth;

Try to put a regular old iamb in that first foot and something just doesn't feel right . . . Why? Because the natural stress of the word "PRINT-ing" tells you that it is the *first* part of the syllable that has to be stressed, not the second. You would never say "printING," would you (unless you were William Shatner as Captain Kirk and had had one too many . . .)? The way the word is pronounced means that you have to use a trochee (stressed, unstressed) in the first foot, instead of an iamb. Like this:

$$/ \quad \smile$$
Printing

But wait! Things are getting even weirder! If you look at the rest of the line, something doesn't feel right again around the word "hooves." It just feels jarring and wrong to your body to unstress the word "hooves," doesn't it? This means that we have to put yet another non-iamb in the third foot of the line. "Hooves" really needs to be stressed. The music of the line falls apart if it is unstressed. Try it both ways and you'll see.

But wait. Oh, dear . . .

This is another one of those extra unstressed beat lines, isn't it? There is no way to shorten anything. Again!

And this is one of those funny epic caesura guys. Do you see it in the third foot? "hooves i' the"? I can try a bunch of different ways to scan the line, but this way—with a dactyl in the third foot—is the way that feels right musically:

$$/ \quad \smile \quad \smile \quad / \quad / \quad \smile\smile \quad \smile \, / \quad \smile \quad /$$
Printing |their proud | **hooves i' th'** |receiv | ing earth;

Thankfully, that last line is a regular old iambic pentameter line. Whew!

Now speak this little piece of text out loud with the interesting scansion we just talked about:

$$\smile \quad / \quad \smile \, / \quad \smile \, / \quad \smile \quad / \quad \smile \, / \quad \smile$$
Think, **when** |we **talk** | of **hor** |ses, **that** | you **see** them

$$/ \quad \smile \quad \smile \quad / \quad / \quad \smile\smile \quad \smile / \quad \smile \quad /$$
Printing |their **proud** | **hooves** i' th' |**receiv** | ing **earth;**

$$\smile \, / \quad \smile \quad / \quad \smile \, / \quad \smile \quad / \quad \smile \quad /$$
For '**tis** |your **thoughts** | that **now** |must **deck** | our **kings**

It should sound like this:

> Think, WHEN we TALK of HORses THAT you SEE them
> PRINTing their PROUD HOOVES i' th' reCEIVing EARTH;
> For 'TIS your THOUGHTS that NOW must DECK our
>   KINGS,

Do you feel how when you identify where the stresses in the language are supposed to be that the piece drives forward? Play with the scansion any other way and it doesn't quite work.

My students often ask me how to know which metrical construction fits in which place. The answer is, your body will tell you what works and what doesn't if you stop and listen. If things flow, it works. If it disrupts the rhythm, keep looking. It's that simple. You will know when it doesn't work because it is difficult to speak the text. When you find the right scansion, the text unfolds smoothly.

This sense of forward motion is incredibly important in all texts, but it is especially so in *this* text, since the words themselves are meant to conjure up the image of galloping horses. Shakespeare does this a lot—he makes the verse a special effect! Speak the verse with the stress in the wrong places and it is feels like those horses are getting stuck in the mud. Identify the rhythmic structure correctly for yourself, and you figure out how to make the music and, in this case, to make those horses gallop into the next lines.

Let's look at one more example. This time Gloucester from *The Tragedy of Richard the Third*:

> Now is the winter of our discontent
> Made glorious summer by this sun of York;
> And all the clouds that low'r'd upon our house
> In the deep bosom of the ocean buried.

Now let's scan it.

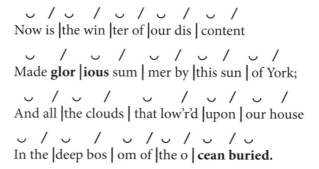

When we do our scansion, we can see that the first line is regular old iambic pentameter. So is the second line, but an interesting thing happens here. To keep the speech humming along in iambic pentameter and to keep the musicality of the verse flowing as well as possible, it would make sense to truncate that word "glorius" from three syllables (GLOHR-eeh-yus) to two syllables (GLOHR-yus).

Speak the first two lines with the different pronunciations of "glorius." You will feel that shortening the word to two syllables and making it fit better into the framework of the iambic pentameter makes the piece flow better. It's a small choice, but one that allows the piece to roll off of your lips and into the casting director's ear smoothly.

And again . . . in that fourth line we have an extra syllable. Yes, it's another feminine ending. Getting the hang of things?

A Word about Blank Feet

Sometimes you'll find that your text is just humming along nicely, and all of a sudden, it stops! Look at this text from *Hamlet* that I have scanned for you. In this speech Hamlet is considering seeking his vengeance on King Claudius, murderer of his father, King Hamlet. Only poor Hamlet is given pause because Claudius is praying:

$\smile\quad / \quad \smile / \quad \smile \quad / \quad \smile / \smile \quad / \quad \smile$
Now might| I do | it, now |'a is | **a-praying**;

$\smile \quad / \quad \smile \quad / \quad \quad \smile / \quad \smile \quad / \quad \smile / \quad \smile$
And now | I'll do't— | and so |a' goes | **to heaven,**

$\quad \smile / \quad \smile / \quad \smile \quad / \quad \quad \smile \quad / \quad \quad \smile \quad /$
And so | am I | [revenged]. | That would | be scann'd:

$\smile / \quad \smile \quad / \quad \quad \smile \quad / \quad \smile \quad / \quad \smile \quad /$
A vill |ain kills | my fath| er, and | for that

$\smile / \quad \quad \smile \quad / \quad \smile \quad / \quad \quad \smile \quad / \quad \smile \quad /$
I, his | sole son | do this | same vill| ain send

$\quad \smile \quad / \quad \smile \quad \quad \smile / \quad \smile / \quad \smile / \quad \smile /$
To heaven. |

I want to bring your attention to two very interesting things.

The first: do you notice the feminine endings of the first and second lines of the speech? There is an interesting slowing down. Hamlet is taking in information. The speech literally slows as he gathers his resources.

The second . . . Do you see how the sixth line is only the single foot (amphibrach) "to heaven"? That's all there is to the line! The meter abruptly stops. Why did Shakespeare do this? Because Hamlet just had a big "uh-oh!" moment. He realizes, "Gee! If I kill my father's murderer right now while he is praying, his soul will go to heaven! That's not what I want! I want him to go to hell . . . Geez. That was a close one, Hamlet. I'd better do this murder thing later!"

It is a major realization. Shakespeare wants you to pause the length of those blank feet. So, count four silent feet in your head. Those silent feet speak more than any text could say!

A Word about Abbreviations

You've seen a couple of these funny-looking words in the text examples that I've given you–strange-looking things like:

th'
do't
i'faith
'tis

And weird abbreviations in sentences like:
> **We'ld** jump the life to come

And:
> Printing their proud hooves **i' th'** receiving earth;

And:
> O time, thou must untangle this, not I,
> It is too hard a knot for me **t' untie.**

What *are* these things?

It's your friendly editor doing some of the scansion work you. These abbreviations let you know that the word in question should be shortened. In a case like "t'untie," it is pronounced just like it sounds, with the "t" functioning like a little springboard to the "untie" part. Treat these abbreviations as you would any modern contraction. We all say words like "don't" and "can't" and "won't" without even thinking about them. These abbreviations are to be dealt with pretty much the same way.

Help! This Is All Too Much and I Want a Cookie!

Oh . . . but by now your head is probably spinning. This is all too much!

And you're right. And yes, you deserve a cookie by now.

Really understanding how to do this work requires in-person study and some time spent with a skilled teacher to guide you. Shakespeare's texts can get a little complicated in some of the plays, and for every nine pieces you encounter where the scansion work is pretty straightforward and clear, there will be one piece with tons of irregularities that has you holding your head in your hands (one monologue from Shakespeare's *Antony and Cleopatra*, which I have spent years trying to scan properly, still stumps me. I used to bring it to my graduate students promising brownies to anyone who could crack it . . . no brownie baking to date).

So this is fascinating, amazing stuff, and if you're starting to be intrigued by Mr. Shakespeare, a little later I'll tell you about some more resources to study all of this in depth, but for now, let's rein it in and highlight *our* modest goals with all of this scansion jazz for your audition. I want you to know what scansion is and have an idea of how to go about it, but I do not expect you to be a scansion Ninja in just a few short pages all on your own. My main goals in showing you all of this is:

- to help you to recognize that your monologue or soliloquy has a driving pulse—I want you to really *feel* that musical pulse as you speak your piece
- as best as your limited scansion prowess may be at this point, to help you to let Mr. Shakespeare steer the ship when it comes to choosing words to stresses
- to allow you to recognize that any switches in meter that you may detect may be an acting clue that something in your character's thought process or tactics has switched
- to help you to see that sometimes you can pronounce words or names using more or fewer syllables than you may at first realize

So don't be overwhelmed. Eat that cookie. And know that if even 20 percent of this is registering with you, then you're getting some new tools under your belt to make some cooler choices with your piece than you would have had otherwise.

Getting Started with Scansion

We've gone through some examples together of other Shakespeare monologues and soliloquies. Now let's try to scan your piece.

Preparation
- Making your piece legible is half the battle! Retype your piece. Make sure that you're copying it faithfully from an excellent edi-

tion. Be certain to copy the lines *exactly* as they appear in the book, especially noting all of the punctuation correctly. Proofread it a few times. A little error can throw you.

- Put several blank lines in between each line of typed text. This will give you enough space to write your scansion above the line. Don't make it all too cramped or you won't be able to read your scansion later.
- Using a pencil with a good eraser (you're going to change your mind about things), try to scan your text. You'll probably be sorry and sad if you use a pen! Attempt to keep things in regular iambic pentameter until you hit a funky place where it doesn't feel like it is all working. When you hit a funky place, try different combinations of the other kinds of feet that we talked about (under "Mr. Iamb's Friends") until something feels right. Please feel free to keep a visual of Mr. Iamb's friends in front of you (it may help you). Our goal is always to keep the meter as regular as we can, only changing things when it just doesn't fit right. Be sure to make dividing lines between each metrical foot. It will help to keep things orderly.
- Read your scansion. Is there a sticky line or two? Revisit those places and try a different way to scan it until it makes sense in your body.

Starting to speak
- Do not try to memorize your monologue/soliloquy until you do your scansion. It will be hard to make new choices once your piece is memorized in a different rhythm.
- Go through your piece a few times in "Scansion Land." Scansion Land is what I call that awkward stage where you sound a little bit like an unstressed/stressed robot. You won't sound like a normal person speaking, and that's okay. What you're doing by speaking in Scansion Land is programing Shakespeare's rhythm into your body, and that's a good thing!
- After you've gone through your text this way about five times, hop the train out of Scansion Land. You won't be in Normal Actorville just yet, but you will be moving to the next station on your journey! Speak the text with an awareness of the scansion, but make it sound a little more like normal speech. Do this about four times.

- If you're a comfortable singer (if singing is fun for you), sing your scansion! First, sing it in Scansion Land using only two notes (one lower note for unstressed beats and one higher note for stressed beats). Then take the train out of Singer Scansion Land and open up the text to other notes, keeping in mind the two-note work that you just did. If you like to sing, this is the fastest, most illuminating way (I have found with my students) to get you using your scansion in a way that feels freeing and fun rather than restrictive!

- Once you've done this work a few times through (either singing or speaking or a combination of both), step away for a little bit, grab dinner, go to the movies, go to sleep and let it sink in before we add the next layer to your piece.

PUNCTUATION AND INFLECTION

The great news is that by now, with all of your scansion work, your piece is probably pretty close to being memorized. Now let's look at a few more tools to help your piece come to life!

"Where am I supposed to breathe?"

This question from my student, asked when she saw her Shakespeare monologue in front of her for the first time, came as a bit of a surprise to me. But the question was one of the most important an actor could ask.

The breath is the thought. We literally, as human beings, take inspiration (breathe in) before we speak. Well, in Shakespeare's world, language was something to be savored. To the Elizabethans, language was of far greater importance than it is to most of us today. Because of this relishing of words, Shakespeare's sentence structures were often much more complicated than today's. Articulated thoughts in Shakespeare's plays are often longer, and his grammars are more complex than we are used to.

So if the breath is the thought, and Shakespeare was a bit "thinkier" in his thoughts than most of us modern folks are used to, where does an actor breathe, and how does she make sense of things?

In music there are logical places to breathe. If you're the singer or if you're playing a brass or wind instrument, the music has small spaces to take a breath. This breath is not only important physically ('cause you're a mammal and you need to breathe!), but the tiny space where the breath is taken gives shape and meaning to what is said next—either in music or in verse. Verse, just like music, tells you where to breathe too. And this is where punctuation comes in . . .

Punctuation, quite simply, tells you when and where to breathe. In addition to this, punctuation also offers suggestions for vocal inflection that will help your text come to life.

We cannot be certain what punctuation Shakespeare used, but great editors have tried to help you in this matter. Let them help you make the most sense out of your piece by following the punctuation road map that they have provided for you.

How to Read the Punctuation Road Map

You know how when you drive your car, a stop sign tells you to stop and a yield sign tells you to yield (okay, unless you live where I used to live in Florida, where these things still meant that you should go whenever you please . . .). So, for most of America, we have road signs like stop signs and yield signs that tell us what to do. Let's think of punctuation marks in Shakespeare as being a bit like road signs; they tell you what to do so that you can handle the conditions ahead.

Here's a little chart to help you to read the Shakespeare road map.

PUNCTUATION AND VOCAL INFLECTION

Kind of Puctuation	How to Handle a Pause or Stop	Kind of Vocal Inflection
.	fully stop	downward ↘
,	brief pause	sustained → or upward ↗
: ; —	slightly longer pause	sustained → or upward ↗
! ?	fully stop	upward ↗

All of these punctuation marks present an opportunity to take a breath if you need it. A period, exclamation point, or question mark is a full stop and a longer breath can be taken here. Other kinds of punctuation can be a catch breath—a brief moment to take in a tiny bit of air if you need it. Take a breath when you need it, and take it on punctuation. It will keep your vocal instrument working well, and it will keep the text making sense.

But let us get back to my strange chart. What does this all mean?

When you see a . in the text, you should fully stop. Your vocal inflection should go down.

Let's use modern examples and give Mr. Shakespeare a breather for a minute.

Say this sentence with a downward vocal inflection (the tone of your voice goes down) and fully stop your energy:

I have a cat ∎

Now let's try the same sentence with slightly different punctuation. When you see a **!** or a **?** in the text, you should also fully stop. But this time your vocal energy should be directed up at the end of the line, in an upward inflection. Try it.

(You just brought Fluffy home from the humane society):
I have a cat!

(Your roommate, without your knowledge, brought Fluffy home from the humane society):
I have a cat?

This is easy stuff, right? Your energy stops. Your voice goes up or down depending on what the punctuation looks like. It's a piece of cake.

But here's where things get tricky and where actors forget what to do . . .

When you see a **,** in the text, you should pause very slightly *and* be very careful not to drop your vocal energy downward but to keep your vocal energy lifted and sustained.

When you see a **:** **;** or a **—** in the text, you should pause, but pause for slightly longer than you would for a comma, being very mindful not to drop your vocal energy.

Let's try it out on Fluffy for a second.

I have a cat named Fluffy; *he's orange and he's awesome* ∎

(You didn't drop your vocal energy on the semicolon right? You paused and kept your vocal energy going, yes? Good stuff!)

This all may look like a minor thing, but believe me, it's huge when it comes to acting your Shakespeare piece.

Do you know that most actors stop their vocal energy all the time on other punctuation and that this is one of the biggest reasons that lots of Shakespeare doesn't make sense?

Do you know that actors are always dropping their vocal inflections downward on punctuation other than periods?

This is a vocal crime that I call "end stopping." *End stopping is stopping the vocal energy by dropping the inflection of your voice when the thought actually needs to continue.* End stopping is the single biggest crime against Shakespeare! When Shakespeare doesn't make sense, chances are, actors are end stopping. You're only allowed to end stop on a period. End of story!

Otherwise, keep your vocal inflection up!

But why is this important? It's important because Shakespeare's verse is often written in huge sentences. I once worked on a two-minute monologue that only had two periods in the whole thing. That meant that if I didn't find a way to keep the energy of the text flowing by keeping my vocal inflection up, the logic of the text wouldn't flow and the audience would lose the meaning. Stopping the vocal energy of the piece when you're not supposed to makes the difference between the audience being able to track the thought and the audience not understanding what's being said. It's that important.

Let's look at an example. Here is Cassius's monologue from *The Tragedy of Julius Caesar*.

> You are dull, Casca; and those sparks of life
> That should be in a Roman you do want,
> Or else you use not. You look pale and gaze,
> And put on fear, and cast yourself in wonder,
> To see the strange impatience of the heavens;
> But if you would consider the true cause
> Why all these fires, why all these gliding ghosts,
> Why birds and beasts from quality and kind,
> Why old men, fools, and children calculate,
> Why all these things change from their ordinance,
> Their natures, and preformed faculties,
> To monstrous quality—why, you shall find
> That heaven hath infus'd them with these spirits,
> To make them instruments of fear and warning
> Unto some monstrous state.

Look at the text. Circle the punctuation. Where is the first period? Play a game with yourself; don't allow your voice to go down until you see that first period. Keep reading. Don't allow your voice to go down until you hit the next period (which doesn't happen for a long, long time)!

Do you see how, when the text does not have punctuation at the end of a line, the thought continues to the next line? This is called an "enjambment." *An enjambment is when there is incomplete syntax at the end of a line and the meaning runs-over from one line to the next.* For you, the actor, it just means that you need to keep the thought going. You do this by not stopping or dropping your vocal energy. Keep your voice lifted up and keep going!

Let's continue on with the game. Circle the rest of the punctuation. Read the text aloud. Focus on pausing very briefly on those dashes and commas. Do not fully stop, and don't let your vocal energy lag until there is final punctuation!

Going "Up the Stairs" and the Parenthetical

Okay, we'll add two more party tricks to the punctuation soirée, and these are what I call "going up the stairs" and the parenthetical.

First, "going up the stairs" because it's so much fun.

Shakespeare loves building lists. He does it all the time in his monologues. Remember how I said that the Elizabethans loved language and that grammar was more complex in Shakespeare's time than it is today? Well, this is what I mean. He can take one idea and build on it and build on it.

Let's look at a modern example, and then we'll go back to the Cassius monologue.

We use lists all of the time. If I were to say to you:

> I'm so mad at you: you didn't do the dishes, you didn't change the roll of toilet paper, you shaved my dog, and you ate all of the Twinkies.

That sentence would pack *way* more of a punch if after each comma, I raised my vocal pitch just slightly, as though I were vocally "going up the stairs." Try it!

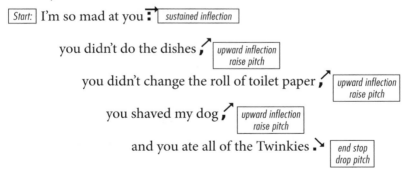

When you separate out each of these thoughts vocally, you increase the tension in the piece; you build excitement and you clarify the text. Say the same text with the same pitch throughout and not only is it kind of boring, but it loses the building of the thoughts.

Let's try it with Cassius. Let's jump to this part, since Shakespeare starts to make a long list here:

> You look pale and gaze,
> And put on fear, and cast yourself in wonder,

To see the strange impatience of the heavens;
But if you would consider the true cause
Why all these fires, why all these gliding ghosts,
Why birds and beasts from quality and kind,
Why old men, fools, and children calculate,
Why all these things change from their ordinance,
Their natures, and preformed faculties,
To monstrous quality—why, you shall find
That heaven hath infus'd them with these spirits,
To make them instruments of fear and warning
Unto some monstrous state.

Shakespeare sets up his thesis statement "You look pale and gaze, And put on fear and cast yourself in wonder, To see the strange impatience of the heavens;" and then he starts to list things. I've broken down the elements of the list for you below:

You look pale and gaze, *(slight pause, raise pitch)*
And put on fear, *(slight pause, raise pitch)*
and cast yourself in wonder, *(slight pause, raise pitch)*
To see the strange impatience of the heavens; *(longer pause, sustained inflection)*
(start this next line at a lower pitch)
But if you would consider the true cause *(enjambment—keep the line going into*
        the next thought)
Why all these fires, *(slight pause, raise pitch)*
Why all these gliding ghosts, *(slight pause, raise pitch)*
Why birds and beasts from quality and kind, *(slight pause, raise pitch)*
Why old men, *(slight pause, raise pitch)*
fools, *(slight pause, raise pitch)*
and children calculate, *(slight pause, raise pitch)*
Why all these things change from their ordinance, *(slight pause, raise pitch)*
Their natures, *(slight pause, raise pitch)*
and preformed faculties, *(slight pause, raise pitch)*
To monstrous quality— *(longer pause, sustained inflection)*

Now, let's combine the list with the rest of the speech. This time, I'll embolden the punctuation and only use the arrows to indicate your vocal inflection:

You are dull**,**   Casca**;** and those sparks of life ↵ *enjambment*
That should be in a Roman you do want**,**
Or else you use not **⟍** You look pale and gaze**,**
And put on fear**,** and cast yourself in wonder**,**

To see the strange impatience of the heavens; →
But if you would consider the true cause ↲ *enjambment*
Why all these fires↗ why all these gliding ghosts↗
Why birds and beasts from quality and kind↗
Why old men↗ fools↗ and children calculate↗
Why all these things change from their ordinance↗
Their natures↗ and preformed faculties↗
To monstrous quality ↩why↗ you shall find
That heaven hath infus'd them with these spirits↗
To make them instruments of fear and warning ↲ *enjambment*
Unto some monstrous state↘

And the last party trick, the "parenthetical" . . .

That is just a fancy way of saying "parentheses." You know those paren-thesis guys . . . they're not so interesting. They're just functional. You know from high school English class that parentheses appear in the sentence to give the reader a little more information. Here's a sentence using parenthe-ses, again with Fluffy the Cat, in case you missed him.

Fluffy (my long-haired orange cat) likes tuna.

If you read that whole sentence with the same vocal inflection, it's hard to separate out the extra information from the primary information. The primary information is that Fluffy likes tuna. The fact that he is long-haired and orange is special bonus information. So read it again with "Fluffy" and "likes tuna" on the same vocal plane, and drop "my long-haired orange cat" down to a slightly lower pitch:

normal pitch	lower pitch	normal pitch
Fluffy	*(my long-haired orange cat)*	*likes tuna.*

Shakespeare employs this construction frequently, only most of the time he (the editor, actually) won't use parentheses. Most of the time Shakespeare's text will be separated by commas, like this:

Fluffy, my long-haired orange cat, likes tuna.

But Shakespeare didn't talk about anything as mundane as Fluffy liking tuna. And if he did want to talk about it, he'd find a much more interesting way to talk about Fluffy's dietary habits than I just did.

Let's look at this tiny piece of text from *Measure for Measure*, for the character Lucio:

I think thou dost; and, indeed, with most painful
feeling of thy speech: I will, out of thine own
confession, learn to begin thy health; but, whilst I
live, forget to drink after thee.

Look at those parentheticals. We can see parentheticals on:

"and, indeed," in the first line
"out of thine own confession," in the second line

I think thou dost; (and,) with most painful feeling of thy speech:
drop pitch (indeed,) *drop pitch even more!*

I will, (out of thy own confession,) learn to begin thy health;
drop pitch

but, (whilst I live,) forget to drink after thee.
drop pitch

and "whilst I live" in the third line
Separate out the extra (parenthetical) information vocally and the text
flows logically!

A Recap of the Punctuation Party

- If you don't pay attention to punctuation, your piece may feel flat
  and boring, and your text probably won't make too much sense to
  your audience
- Punctuation tells you where to breathe. Breathe fully on full-
  stop punctuations like . ! ? and you can take a catch breath on
  ; : — or ,
- Pay attention to your vocal inflection. Allow your voice to go down
  only on a period. Otherwise, use a sustained or upward vocal inflection.
  End-stopping is a crime against Shakespeare! If you keep the thought
  in the air vocally until, and only until, reaching the final punctuation,
  the text will make sense and be easily understood by the listener.
- When you see lists of things that build, also build the ideas vocally.
  Do this by vocally "going up the stairs."
- Treat parenthetical information by altering your pitch. This will separate out the thoughts, making it easier for your audience to understand. Laura, your Shakespeare author, thinks that this will help you
  have a better audition.

Getting Started with Punctuation and Inflection

As you learn your piece, let's explore its punctuation and vocal inflection. To do this:

- Make a copy of your piece that is separate from the copy you were using to work on your scansion. Double and triple check that you have correctly copied your editor's punctuation.
- Circle all of the punctuation your editor has given you.
- Draw arrows on the page to help you remember what you should do with your voice.
  - Draw a downward arrow for periods (to remind you that your vocal inflection should go down).
  - Draw an upward arrow for any exclamation points or question marks (to remind you to lift your voice up).
  - Draw a straight or an upward arrow above any dashes, colons, semicolons, or commas to remind you to use a sustained inflection and not to end-stop or drop your vocal energy.
  - Draw a line under any parenthetical constructions to remind you to separate out that thought vocally and to make it vocally distinctive.
- Read your piece several times through, thinking only about the punctuation and inflection.
- Repeat this until your new vocal choices and pauses start to become automatic.

The work you did on your scansion will probably be in your body by now. While you're working on punctuation and inflection, you don't need to focus on scansion. In fact, if you focus on punctuation and let the scansion go a little, it will probably still retain its framework but settle into a more natural way of speaking for you.

If this is not the case, I would suggest going through your piece a few times, focusing alternately on scansion and then on punctuation. Do this for a while . . . And then . . . *let it go!*

12. Putting It All Together

You have a lot of tools now.

You've conquered your fear, you have a great editor working for you, you found the right piece, you know the play and your given circumstances, you know who you are talking to and what you need, and you have a basic understanding of meter and how to use punctuation and inflection to make your piece dynamic.

What's next?

At the end of the last chapter I gave you a very unusual direction. I said, "let it go."

At a certain point, you've done the homework. Most of it will stick without your thinking about it. So now that you've thought about it so much, it's time to stop thinking about it!

The great director Anne Bogart once said, "do your homework and know when to stop doing your homework" (Bogart 2003)

It's time to stop doing your homework and to *play*.

Warm up your body and your voice. Find an open space. Visualize your imaginary scene partner in the room and get what you need from them. That is your mission.

Ways to Play

Here are some ideas to help you play. These are rehearsal exercises designed to free you up as you explore your piece. Only do the ones that appeal to you and that sound like fun to you! After all, you already did all of the hard work. Now it's playtime!

Do the piece with arbitrary tempo shifts.
- Speak some parts of your piece very quickly; speak other parts slowly. Speak other parts at tempos in between. What do you find?
- Do it again and switch it around.
- Do it a third time, not being conscious of the tempo. Which discoveries did you keep?

Sing your piece like it's an opera aria. What discoveries do you make?
- Sing the piece *forte*.

- Sing it again *piano.*
- Sing it with many different vocal dynamics.
- Now alternate between singing and speaking the piece. Sing a few lines, then go back and speak those lines. What did you discover?

Your monologue is your crazy modern dance piece. Physicalize it. What do you find?

- Speak the piece and move all over the space, using huge, exaggerated physical gestures.
- Do the piece once through in complete stillness.
- Do the piece a third time mixing moments of movement and moments of stillness. What do you discover?

Explore the consonant sounds in the piece.

- Go through the piece focusing on the muscularity of sounds. Do you have a bunch of "b" or "p" sounds in a row? What is the quality of these sounds? Does your piece have a bunch of "f" and "v" sounds, or "m" and "l" sounds? How are the sounds different? How do they feel different in your mouth? How do they feel different psychologically? Draw out the sounds; enjoy them. Make some short and some long.
- Speak the text again without focusing consciously on the sounds. What discoveries did you retain?

Once you have fun playing with any of these ideas, keep what want to keep, and let the rest go. All of these ideas are here to help you to get into your body and to get out of your head after so much intellectual work. So— enjoy the process and don't take it too seriously. If any of these exercises make you feel like you're overthinking, let them go and try something else.

Above all, do not "set" how you are going to perform your piece. What's the fun of that? You have the basic framework now. Once you have the framework, there's so much room for variation and discovery in the work. Find it all fresh and in the moment! Your auditioners will thank you for it.

13. Some Thoughts about Your Audition

*A*h, audition day.

You've done so much work for this day.

But you know what? It's just a day . . .

So let's just a few hit a few key points so that all of your hard work can be seen to its best advantage.

You may be relatively new to auditions, or you may be seasoned at auditioning for contemporary plays; no matter your level of expertise in an audition room, it never hurts to be reminded of some basics. There are lots of great books written about audition skills (the best, in my mind, being Michael Shurtleff's quintessential book *Audition*. Check it out if you haven't already. It's a must for every serious actor).

Our purpose in *this* book is more about preparing you to do the work needed to select material and to prepare your text for your audition than about the audition day itself, but like a grandma telling you not to go out without your sweater, dear, here are a few important reminders:

Be yourself. Okay, everybody says that, and it's one of those things that's easier said than done. Don't feel like you're supposed to be someone you're not to please other people. For starters, wear what you feel like you in. I remember when I first moved to New York and began going to auditions. For some reason, every musical theatre actor in New York wore a jewel-toned wrap dress and had beige character shoes . . . "Oh geez, I need to go out and buy a jewel-toned wrap dress and some beige character shoes . . ." I panicked. No! I did not! I look lousy in jewel-toned wrap dresses. It took me a while to embrace being me instead of worrying that I should be something else. But it was good to be me. Be you. Wear something simple with clean lines that you feel good in. Get your hair out of your face so people can see you. Keep your accessories simple. Make your audition about you, not about what you're wearing. Be your authentic, put-together self.

Don't let other actors freak you out. I can be calm, cool, and collected for an audition, and then I walk into the waiting room to sign in and all of that nervous actor energy is vibrating in the air and I start to catch their freakiness. "Haaahhh. Hahhhhh. (lip trill, lip trill, lip trill). Toy boaT, Toy boaT.

Toy boaT. Haaaaahhhhhh, EEEEeeehhhh . . ." says nervous actor number twenty four with his hands on his diaphragmatic support. Will you warm up at *home*, people? This is nerve-racking and weird! You've probably been there too. Don't let their nervousness become your nervousness. After all, you're really prepared, right? You have this thing! So tune them out. I always try to step slightly outside of the waiting room; just close enough where I am sure to hear them call my name when it's time for them to see me, and just far enough away not to become a part of the fear circus.

You know this, of course, but remember to bring your résumé and headshot (and eat your vegetables). In all of this excitement it's easy to forget, and as an actor you never ever want to find yourself résumé-less. Have your résumé with you at all times when you're an actor. And always have more than one. I personally am prone to spilling tea on mine.

When it's your time to go into the audition room, be warm and be professional. I've seen all of the extremes, from actors that are too chilly to actors that are too chatty. Be delightful and get down to work. Always take your cue from the people who are auditioning you. If they get up to shake your hand and say, "I'm Bill, the artistic director and this is Fred, our musical director," shake their hands and tell them it's nice to meet them, but do not initiate such things. Reciprocate warmly, but never initiate. I will never forget once when I was casting a show, an actor came up to the table and kissed me on the cheek as he gave me his résumé and said, "Nice to meet you, darling." His audition was over before he ever opened his mouth to speak! Keep a nice cushion of space between you and the people who are auditioning you, unless you are invited in any way to narrow that space. Pretend that there is an invisible force field up between you and them. Only they have the superpowers to cross through the force field or to invite you to cross through it. I've seen so many actors who come too close to the audition table, and believe me, when you're the one doing the casting, actors who come too close make you feel uncomfortable and awkward. The people behind the table want to be able to objectively see you and your work. Help them to do this.

Introducing your piece, believe it or not, is pretty darn important. Why? Because it's a way for the people auditioning you to get a feel, quick though it may be, for the *real* you before you launch into your piece. Please, please, I beg you, do not be an "Introduction Robot." "My name is Casey Brown and I will be performing blah blah blah, boring, fake, boring". So many acting teachers do actors a disservice by telling them how to "slate" themselves. Yes, if it is a big cattle-call audition where you are given a number to wear like in a 1950s dance-a-thon, it's kind of hard not to say your name, rank, and serial number like an automaton when it's your minute and a half to shine, but if you're in a room with other people in it, be a *person*. The conversation might go like this:

> Casting director: "Hi, Casey! What do you have for us today?"
>
> Actor: "Hi! Thanks for seeing me today. I have Edmund from *Lear*."

Do you see how much more human that is? Just by simply introducing your piece like you, the people auditioning you can get a little bit of a feel for what you'd be like to work with. Honestly, being nice to work with is even more important than being the world's best actor. I would rather work with a decent actor who's fabulous to work with than a gifted one who's a big pain. Be the nice actor. When you say it's nice to meet them, when you introduce your pieces, or when you thank them for seeing you on your way out the door, be brief and be genuinely warm. Also, you don't have to give a ton of information when introducing your piece for a Shakespeare audition. Notice that imaginary Casey didn't say "*King Lear*,". They know "*Lear*" is *King Lear*! And notice how imaginary Casey didn't say, "by William Shakespeare." They *know* who wrote the dang play! If an actor tells me Shakespeare's name in an audition when they're introducing their piece, I either think that they are a little slow or that they think that I am. (Oh, and out of respect for those who are superstitious, if you're auditioning with a piece from *Macbeth*, call it *The Scottish Play*. It's just good theatre etiquette even if you personally don't believe in curses on plays. Many people I've worked with that take this curse very seriously. And auditions are hard enough–why tempt the evil eye?)

When you start your piece, ground yourself. Take four or five seconds to see the imaginary place that you are in during the piece and to smell the smells and hear the sounds of that world. Picture who you're talking to before you speak to them. Taking five seconds to do this helps you to get into the world and the auditioners to change their gears to join you in that world.

If you're doing one of those absolutely dreadful timed auditions (which often happen in group calls and auditions for graduate schools) remember, less is more! If the piece should be no more than one minute and thirty seconds, aim for a forty-five-second audition. There's nothing worse than panicking about time while doing your piece. Well, actually, there is! Having a stage manager with a stopwatch call, "Time!" in the middle of it. That's actually worse. Always aim for the too-short rather than the too-long audition. This actually applies to non-timed auditions also. Always leave people wanting more. Leave the Monologue Party while the party is still good. Don't wait for the beer to run out before making your exit.

Where do you look? As we've said, not at the casting director. Do not ever use a casting director or any other associates in the audition room as your scene partner unless expressly invited to do so. We spoke earlier about placing your imaginary partner (whether it be another character or characters, or an aspect of yourself) along the back wall of the audition room. Although it would seem logical to put the imaginary person on stage with you just as you would in a play, resist the urge to do this. In an audition situation, putting your imaginary person on stage with you cuts people off from you. Aim to put your imaginary person at nearly eye level with the people casting you, but do not make eye contact. Grazing the auditioners' ears with your gaze is a great way to go. If you aim your gaze too low, they'll be cut off from seeing you; if you aim your gaze too high, they're looking up your hairy nostrils. Include them, but don't involve them in your piece. They want to see you!

Have fun. Seriously. If you have fun, you will have a good audition. I see so many actors in auditions who look like the experience is painful. They just want to get through it. But when I see an actor who is free on stage and who is playing, that actor is a breath of fresh air. I have fun because they're having fun. What exactly do I mean by fun? It doesn't always mean the piece is light. Being Lady Macbeth is fun! Being Iago is fun! Being Aaron from *Titus Andronicus* is fun. All of these roles are the antithesis of light and airy, but there's so much to play with in Shakespeare's darkness too.

This audition, believe it or not, is not the be-all/end-all of your life. It's just the thing that you are doing today. As an actor, you will have so many auditions; some of them will go great, some of them will be less than great. The important thing is to go in knowing that you're prepared. Preparation is all. You did your homework and you did it well. Now let go and go on the ride! I bet if you make the decision to let go of needing to do it right or well, and just decide to get in there and play, you'll be great.

Have fun.

It's what Shakespeare would have wanted.

14. An Actor Q&A

*M*y acting students are always my barometers. They help me to make sure that I'm giving you the information that you need to do your best work. So I asked my contemporary acting class at San Francisco State University what questions they had about classical auditions. The bulk of their questions were about finding material and how to understand the language–things that I hope I helped you to get a handle on. Here are a few of their questions that we didn't really talk about yet, and here are my responses. Maybe some of their questions will be the same things you've been wondering about.

What are they looking for from a Shakespeare monologue?
Well, for starters, "they" (the people who are auditioning you) are just people. Different people are always looking for slightly different things, because everyone has different tastes, perspectives, and needs. But I think it is safe to say that whoever is auditioning you is looking to see how you connect and communicate, just as they would in any audition situation. The people in the audition room really want to see you have a relationship with whomever you are talking to on stage. They want to see you needing something from that person, and they want to see you trying to get what you need in a way that is clear, honest, and imaginative. In short, they want you to make them care about you.

When you need to do a classical-text audition, are there any alternatives, besides doing a Shakespeare piece?
Yes! Classical material need not only be Shakespeare. You could choose work from any of Shakespeare's contemporaries: Ben Jonson, Christopher Marlowe, Thomas Kyd, or John Webster are all fair game. You could also choose text from an ancient Greek play (though be sure to find a good translations—translations vary greatly). If you're not up for Shakespeare, in my opinion, your next best bet is the French playwright Molière (Jean-Baptiste Poquelin). Molière wrote in verse and is considered to be one of the greatest masters of comedy in western literature. Read a little bit about Molière, watch a video production of one of his plays so that you're sure you understand the style (there is a great Circle in the Square production of Molière's satire *Tartuffe* available on video). But above all, find a good translation of Molière. Not all of them retain their rhyme scheme, and to me, unrhyming Molière is just, well . . . sad. I highly recommend the translations by Richard Wilbur.

Keep in mind what you're auditioning for. For a training situation, you can be equally well served by any of these choices. If you're auditioning for a season in a theatre that contains a Shakespeare play, best to really do a Shakespeare piece.

Should I perform my Shakespeare piece with an accent? (This question came up a few times . . .)
Oh, good Lord, no! Please use your own voice. There is a huge temptation to speak with some hint of a British dialect (mostly because so many great Shakespearean actors are British and this is what our ear gets used to hearing), but unless you are British yourself, don't do it!

There are cases where a Shakespeare role will require a dialect (for instance, this past summer I coached an actor in French dialect who was playing Caius in *The Merry Wives of Windsor*). If you were being called in to audition specifically for this role, then and only then could you prepare something that would showcase this skill. But generally speaking, not only is it not necessary to speak in any kind of dialect for your audition, but it is hugely in the way. Allow the people who are auditioning you to see *you*.

Should you stick to roles within your own gender, or can you expand and experiment?
We touched on this a bit in the Finding Your Match section, where we talked about the romances in particular having some gender flexibility—but it's a big question, so let's go a little bit deeper. If we're looking outside of the flexibility of the romances, this question has one of those "it depends" answers. It really depends on the tastes and views of who is auditioning you. When I was auditioning actors for a graduate program that I used to teach at, I saw a sea of unmemorable Juliets, Lady Annes, and Portias . . . but I will never forget the girl who had the chutzpah enough to be Hamlet. As cool as Shakespeare's women are, I think nothing tops his writing for his men. Beatrice and Rosalind are amazing, but they ain't no Hamlet. So for me, it works. But for some people, it may not. I say if your audition is for graduate schools or training programs, or for a theatre that you know is hip, edgy, risk-taking, and gender-bendy, go for it! Be a lady Macbeth (not just Lady Macbeth). Be a female Iago if it fits the bill. If it is for a traditional kind of theatre company for a specific role, play within your own gender to help them to see your casting possibilities better. Gauge the situation and go with your gut.

What are the most commonly mispronounced words in Shakespeare auditions?

Oh, what a great question! There are few things more jarring to the ear than mispronounced words in your audition. Always refer to the pronunciation guides that I suggested earlier, especially for people and place names. That said, here are some of the top mispronounced words that I hear (that make me cringe) and the way that they should be pronounced:

> troth (pronounce this word to rhyme with "oath")
> bade (take off that pesky ending "e" and pronounce it like "bad")
> dost (pronounce like the word "dust")
> doth (pronounce like "duhth")
> i' (joined to another word) like 'i faith (pronounce this like "ih" and make it a launching point to the main word that it is joined to)
> err (we probably think it should sound like "air" but it actually should be pronounced "urr")

You will encounter these words above very often, so best to build good pronunciation habits now. (Oh, and, this is very specific, but if I had a dime for every time an actor mispronounced the word "surfeited" (SIR-fitted), well, paying back those graduate school loans wouldn't look quite so daunting . . .)

How should I move when I perform the piece?

The answer: however the language tells you to move. One of the biggest mistakes I see actors make (and a mistake that I made myself as a young actor) is coming up with a predetermined, intellectual decision about how you will move–an "I'm going to walk forward and raise my arms on this line" kind of a thing. Don't do it! Don't plan! Don't feel like you have to move for the sake of moving. Let the language engage your instrument. Such visceral language will certainly find expression in your body that is natural and organic. Don't force anything to happen; simply allow it to happen.

Should I wear something specific for a classical audition?

I've seen way too many Elizabethanesque puffy shirts in my time. It is like the pirate convention let out early or there was an after-Halloween sale at Joanne Fabric. You don't need to look all "Renaissance Fair" for your audition, okay? So put away that sewing kit. Wear what you would wear for any other kind of audition; simple clothes in basic colors that showcase you and that allow you to move freely. Tie your hair back so people can see your expressive face. Wear flattering yet sensible shoes, and let the text be your jewelry.

How do I prepare for a callback situation?

In a callback situation for a Shakespeare play, most likely you will be given some time with the audition sides (advanced copies of the script) for the role you are being seen for. If you're lucky, you'll be called back for a show where the director and company are using a well-edited, coherent version of the text, even if it has been cut for time. If the text looks pretty well intact, go for it and do your scansion work. Scan your own lines as well as the other characters' lines; that way you can see how everything fits together. If you have time, it is always, always better to go in to your callback off-book (but sometimes time does not allow for this). Do it if at all possible.

If you are a little less lucky, the show you are being called back for may have a hacked up text. Companies that cut Shakespeare plays down due to time concerns often don't cut them skillfully; they bust up meter and make a real wreck of the joint. Sadly, this happens more often than not. Do the best you can, but realize that your scansion work may have some limitations. And (this comes from someone who has had to bite her lower lip an awful, awful lot . . .) resist pointing out to the folks in charge, even once you get the job, that their text is chopped up and doesn't scan. It is so, so tempting when dealing with a messy text to want to fix something that will make your job easier, but your knowledge won't make you popular. Grin and bear it. And go to the bar afterward. No one wants you to be a smarty-pants except your mom.

15. What's Next?

If you're anything like most of my students, once you get past the fear and get a little bit of a handle on Shakespeare, not only do you start to *not* dread it . . . you start to love it.

So, what do you do now? Where do you get more training? How do you get more intimate with Mr. Shakespeare? I suggest two avenues: self-study and formal training.

While it is always wonderful to have the experience of intensive on-your-feet study (and really, nothing can compare to the experience of working in an ensemble environment with other actors and a great teacher), it isn't always possible given the other demands of life. If you'd like to continue to learn more about Shakespeare, the number of resources out there is truly overwhelming. There are so many books written from a scholarly perspective–too many to count. There are also tons of acting resources out there. So here are just a few of my favorites. These are resources that really help actors:

Playing Shakespeare, John Barton
This video master class from the Royal Shakespeare Company includes work from actors Judi Dench, Ian McKellen, Patrick Stewart, Ben Kingsley, and David Suchet, and may have some dated clothing and strange sideburns, but will never go out of style. It's 456 minutes of mind-blowing Shakespeare acting and incredibly insightful text analysis. If you are at all serious about Shakespeare, watch this!

The Working Shakespeare Collection: A Workbook for Teachers, Cicely Berry
A wonderful book that deals with language, subtext, and sound.

Speak the Speech: Shakespeare's Monologues Illuminated, Rhona Silverbush and Sami Plotkin
A fantastic resource for future auditions! This book highlights a wide range of monologues and not only includes very useful dramaturgical information, but highlights irregular scansion issues and other potential pitfalls in your chosen piece.

How to Do Shakespeare, Adrian Noble
This book delves into rhythmic and linguistic patterns in Shakespeare. Clearly written from a director's point of view.

Speaking Shakespeare, Patsy Rodenburg
An excellent book that investigates vocal choices, verse structure, and rhetorical forms.

If you have time in your life for some concentrated, in-person training, well, that is always an amazing opportunity for growth. Most graduate acting programs have a substantial classical training component, but if an advanced degree really isn't in your plan, there are other ways to get excellent training.

You will find that the bulk of great non-degree-granting Shakespeare intensives are geared toward gifted high school students: great news if you are a gifted high school student, a little disappointing if you're not.

At the very top of my list for serious actors, because of its unique combination of terrific quality, good price tag, and intensive yet short training period, is American Conservatory Theatre's (A.C.T.) Summer Training Congress. A.C.T offers a five-week program in core acting skills as part of their Summer Training Congress. In addition to the five-week course is a two-week Shakespeare training intensive that can be done in combination with the five-week summer intensive or on its own. In the Shakespeare intensive, actors focus on the specific craft of performing Shakespeare and other classical texts. Visit www.actsf.org/home/conservatory/summer_training_congress.html to learn more about the programs. This could be a great next step in your development as an actor.

Hopping across the pond, the Royal Academy of Dramatic Art (RADA) Summer Shakespeare School could be great fun for you. Check out their website at www.rada.ac.uk.

Massachusetts-based Shakespeare and Company is a highly respected home for Shakespeare's work in performance and education. While their teachings and views of Shakespeare training clash with my own training and the techniques that I teach and use, I have had many students report worthwhile and freeing experiences there. You might want to check them out at www.shakespeare.org/training.

Whether you have a quick and dirty affair with Mr. Shakespeare and just get through your audition in one semi-confident piece, or you are just beginning a lifelong romance with the world's greatest playwright, I hope you discovered that Shakespeare can be great fun.

I hope that through the beauty and truth of his words you found some new part of yourself that you shared with a roomful of strangers; and I hope that you made some new discoveries, uncovered some new truths, and made a chilly audition room come warmly and vibrantly alive—even for a moment—as you ignited your soul and your auditioners'.

Prof. Laura Wayth is available for audition coaching via skype.

Please contact her at San Francisco State University at lwayth@sfsu.edu, subject line "Shakespeare coaching."

Bibliography

"The Complete Works of William Shakespeare." Jeremy Hylton. Web 1993.

"Heighten." Merriam-Webster, n.d. Web 2015.

"How Shakespeare's Plays Found Print." Michael J. Cummings. Web 2003.

"Online Etymology Dictionary." Douglas Harper. Web 2014.

"Shakespeare Life and Times." M.Alan Kazlev. Web 2004.

"Shakespearean Verse and Prose." Debora B. Schwartz. Web 2015.

Bogart, Anne. 2003. *A Director Prepares*. New York: Routledge.

Epstein, Norrie. 1993. *The Friendly Shakespeare*. New York: Penguin.

Evans, G. Blakemore, et al. 1997. *The Riverside Shakespeare*.
    New York: Houghton Mifflin.

Index